C000163492

The House of Prayer

I dedicate this book to St Joseph's House of Prayer and
to all the friends
and benefactors who have
helped the House to become
what it now is:
A House of Prayer

JOSEF PICHLER

The House of Prayer
Praying Contemplatively

FOUNT

An imprint of HarperCollins Publishing

First published in Great Britain in 1991 by Fount Paperbacks.

Fount Paperbacks is an imprint of
Collins religious Division,
Part of the HarperCollins Publishing Group
77–85 Fulham Palace Road, London W6 8JB

Printed and bound in Great Britain by
Cox & Wyman Ltd, Reading

Contents

ACKNOWLEDGEMENTS

For the basic ideas in Parts 2 to 8 I am indebted to a series of typescript booklets by Werner-Egon Gross O.F.M. Cap., entitled *Kontemplation, was ist das?*

For the basic method of praying the Scriptures in Part 9, I am indebted to a booklet by Peter Dodson entitled *Towards Contemplation* (Fairacres, Oxford).

For techniques of becoming aware of breathing, touching and listening I am indebted to Anthony de Mello *Sadhana – A way to God* (St Louis Jesuits, 1973), and in a few cases the meditations have been influenced by his ideas.

The Bible Version used throughout is the Revised Standard Version (RSV).

Foreword

Meditative prayer has increasingly struck a chord in the lives of many people. Books have appeared during the past few years which have given us a variety of explanations and ways into the inner life as well as a good deal of theory. However, I do not recall finding a book quite like this.

The author of this very practical guide is Father Joe Pichler who founded the House of Prayer at Burn Hall in Durham. He writes from first-hand experience over many years with those who have sought spiritual help and guidance there. All that you will read in the following pages has worked with actual groups and individuals. So everyone can find much benefit in following the guidance most in tune with their needs, knowing that others have also been helped.

This book will be of support and encouragement to individuals and to groups, to those who are experienced and to those who are just beginning to seek the way. There is something here for everyone. Taste and see.

J. Hampson

Introduction

The value of praying contemplatively became clear to me after an experience I had in my student days in Mill Hill. We used to go out in threes or fours and I once found myself in a group that wanted to go to an Art Gallery. When we arrived I went through all the galleries looking right and left, never stopping till I reached the very end. I saw most of the pictures hanging on the walls to be sure, but only with a passing glance. When I came back to where we had started I found that one of my companions was still at the first picture and that the others were only at the fourth or fifth. What had happened? They were really taking each picture into their *hearts*. They looked at it from all angles, noting all the little details. They truly entered into the mind of the artist and discovered the message the picture was portraying. As for me, I had seen a lot of pictures but benefited very little from the experience.

I became aware of a similar pattern of behaviour in my reflections on the natural world and in my travels. I saw all the beauty of God's creation, dales, mountains and rivers. I noticed all the different flowers, even the tiny ones, as well as the birds and animals. Yet I hardly ever took a flower in my hand to finger its petals, enjoy its perfume or allow myself to marvel at and be touched by it. With the passage of time I am trying to alter this pattern, and am becoming better at it, very gradually.

Now, when we pray we also find ourselves in a most wonderful Art Gallery, the gallery of our heart. Jesus says: "When you pray, go into your room and shut the door and pray to the Father in secret" (Matthew 6:6). This Art Gallery is very special, for there we can be totally alone with God. It is his dwelling place and we find there many pictures of Christ's life on display, though we do not always see them. The important thing is not to gaze at too many pictures but to focus on one and to spend as much time as possible on that. Look at the whole picture, see it from different angles, enjoy it, love it, allow yourself to be captivated by it and even to become part of it. To do this, of course, we must set aside sufficient time and be interiorly free from pressures, we must try to relax and be at peace. We must not have any great plans or expectations but rather be content to dwell on one picture, one mystery of our faith, for as long as possible. This is what we mean by praying contemplatively. Such prayer can really transform us if we can manage to practise it regularly with persistence, and not be put off by patches of possible aridity which may come to us all from time to time. For are we not supposed to become like Christ? Christ is the picture, we are his images.

My attraction to the art galleries has not changed very much down the years, but now, thanks be to God, I can stay within my heart focusing on one image for a long time. Even in dryness and emptiness I can still contemplate Jesus "my mother, my brother, my saviour" (Julian of Norwich). With a little effort you can do the same and thereby find your prayer life deepened and enriched.

With this present book I am offering you a manual that contains several ways of praying contemplatively, each with a number of examples to choose from. For we are all different. We don't fit into the same mould, we need variety, and each one of us must find a form that appeals to him or her individually. The book contains nine ways of praying. It might be helpful to read through them all first and see which one would suit you best. Then choose that particular one and stay with it. For instance, if you choose number three, "Praying with One Word", you will find several examples. Again, read through, or try out, all the examples and then pick the one you like and stay with that Word for several days or weeks or months — perhaps years or even for the rest of your life.

It may be that after some time you would like to change because your relationship with the Lord has changed, has grown, has become more intimate. So you may want a new word: that's fine. But do not continually change the word just because you fancy it. If you pick another way of praying, a more imaginative one, for instance Parts Five to Eight, you will have to change more often. You may need a different scene or event every day. But even here I would say that depth is better than quantity; not the novelty but the intensity. (You may at a later time like to go on to choose your own words and scenes from the Bible and find your particular way of praying these texts.) The order of the chapters is not particularly important as they all stand more or less on their own.

So may the Holy Spirit guide you, and through the use of this book help you to grow into a deeper prayer life, gradually becoming more God-centred in the whole of your life.

Preface

When I pray I try to place myself first in the presence of God, or rather, I try to become consciously *aware* of God's presence. I know quite well that he is present everywhere for God is in all things and all things are in him. He is in a very special way present in me, in my heart, as he is in everyone who is open to him. Julian of Norwich says: that God has made in my heart his resting place and glorious city, a throne from which he will never rise, nor ever leave. So in order to pray we don't need to go anywhere special except into our hearts.

For me prayer is just being with the Lord. I know he loves me beyond all telling.

I always begin by invoking the Holy Spirit and asking him to do the praying in me for I do not know how to do it. The Holy Spirit knows how to pray without words, so I can relax and let things happen, let my praying be the way he wants it.

Through the years I have learned that there are many ways to be with the Lord in prayer. The Holy Spirit is really ingenious. He knows where we are at and so he can help us with various different ways of being with the Lord and communicating with him. This applies to all of us whether we are new to prayer or old hands at it.

The first thing to do is always to be still and to listen. God is always the first in prayer. He speaks to us, he touches us and moves us. After that we can respond in many different ways according to the inspiration of the Holy Spirit and where he leads me.

So, I may choose a word or an event, take it to heart and stay with it, savour and ponder it. This can go on and on and on. Or I may want to enjoy and experience the presence of the Lord through my inner senses of seeing, hearing touching or speaking.

These wonderful faculties of ours are very helpful in prayer. Through the imagination we can really see, hear, touch and speak with the Lord. Or again, we may just want to communicate with him through our breathing. Or again, we may want to be wiith the Lord in absolute silence, just being there with him, doing absolutely nothing. There are numerous ways in which we can be with the Lord who loves us so much and whom we want to try to love in return, like two lovers who discover ever new forms of being together.

There are, of course, plenty of challenges. One is not always on cloud nine; often quite the opposite is true. I often feel something like a wall, a darkness, an emptiness or even a vicious image before me that prevents me from coming into God's presence, or rather, from having the sense that I am in his presence. And this obstacle is very real. Yet I know quite well and I also believe that God is there, he is in the very depth of my being, in its very centre and source. I therefore tackle this obstacle, what-ever it may be, with the "dart of longing love". Julian of Norwich says: "The soul can do no more than seek, suffer and trust . . . the seeking with faith, hope and love pleases our Lord, and the finding pleases the soul and fills it full of joy. And it is his will that we seek him until we behold him." So, even our struggle in prayer is moving us closer to God, though it may not feel like it at the time.

The purpose of this book, which has grown out of many years of practical experience, is to offer a number of practical ways of being with the Lord and communicating with him in a personal manner. Most of the prayer exercises I have practised with the prayer group in the House of Prayer in Durham where I work. They are all examples of how we can make use of the religious words and images of our Christian tradition.

They are meant to encourage, stimulate and inspire but not to be used slavishly. Your mood and needs will vary but I hope you will pick up something of value, like a grain of wheat, from one or other of the prayer exercises I describe, and in quiet reflection allow it to speak to you, to touch you and to transform you.

This can profitably be done in union with breathing. At the beginning one often prefers or even needs a longer text to chew on, but gradually, one needs less and less to chew on, until eventually one word or thought will suffice. God may even allow us to behold him, there nothing is needed any more, as then the pray-er is totally satisfied with simply being with him.

In this simple being with the Lord and feeling ever more one with him, we will also discover that we are all brothers and sisters, that we are all related to one another and that we are even related to the whole of creation. One with God makes us one with one another and with the whole of creation. The power of God that lives in us, which is the Holy Spirit, will transform us. It can therefore be said of those people who are true pray-ers: "You are the light of the world" (Matthew 5:14).

As a conclusion to this introduction I would like to express my sincere gratitude and thanks to all the people who, in one way or another, have contributed to the making of this book. There are too many to mention individually but very special thanks are due to Father James Cowan MHM and Sister Una Breen who did the main proof-reading and correcting of the various parts; as well as the many other people who did some proof-reading; to Mrs Carmel Brown, who typed the various parts many times; and to all the people of the contemplative prayer groups with whom I was allowed to share these prayer experiences through the years.

Josef Pichler

PART ONE

A Few Practical Hints . . .

SILENCE AND SOLITUDE

If we do not learn to keep silent before God we shall not make much progress in prayer as God usually communicates himself to us only when we are silent. Remaining silent is hard, it is much easier just to speak to God. If, however, we speak to God without first remaining silent there is a real risk that we shall be speaking only to ourselves and not to God. We must never start off on our prayer by "praying". Silence must precede all prayer and this silence must affect us totally – mind, heart, soul and body. If there is anything making us tense we must try to free ourselves from it, although I appreciate this is not always easy. If it helps, sit or even lie down until you have become completely relaxed. St John of the Cross says: "The Holy Spirit enlightens the mind when it is recollected, and he enlightens it to the extent that it is recollected."

But how can we become recollected? St Teresa of Avila says: "We should seek a quiet place, kneel down, close our eyes, forget the outer world and direct our inner gaze towards God." It is not always as simple as that, as most of us lead busy lives with all sorts of things harassing us. We therefore need some effective techniques. Here are a few suggestions.

21

– Choose a quiet place. Ideally there should be complete silence, but we also have to learn to live with noise and pray during it.
– Choose a lonely place – in front of a cross in a quiet church or room – or a quiet, lonely place outside.
– Try to create a prayerful atmosphere – a dim light – a candle burning – half-closed curtains – soft light music.

POSTURE

What modern psychology tries to impress on us is something long practised by wise people from the East in ages past. Our activities are always holistic, that is, the whole person is involved. The posture of the body is as much an expression of prayer as an intensification of our inner attitude, so prayerful attitude of the body will help create true prayerfulness.

What bodily posture might we adopt? There are many possibilities. Kneeling is a true expression of adoration but on the whole it does not allow us to be quiet and restful for any length of time. Some people prefer to sit back on their heels when kneeling, or to sit on a small stool in such a way that they can adopt a kneel-sit position. We can also pray and meditate when standing up or walking about but neither of these leads us easily into deep prayer.

For most of us the following posture is perhaps the best and most practical. Take a chair or hard stool. The chair should be neither too high nor too low. The feet should rest comfortably on the floor. Do not lean against the back, but if you do, the back should be quite straight. Always sit up straight but in a relaxed fashion. Lay your

hands on your knees, the palms facing upwards, mouth
and eyes closed. Ensure that you are at ease. This posture, like any other, must be practised for some time until
we feel that we can sit quietly and motionless, without
discomfort for a considerable length of time in deep
silence. After having settled down in a comfortable posture we must relax. It is only when we become entirely
still and silent that we notice how tense and harassed we
are. There are countless exercises that help us relax, a
few of which I shall describe later.

BREATHING

All the great masters of prayer know the importance of
correct breathing and recommend the saying of short
ejaculatory prayers following the rhythm of breathing.

The influence of correct breathing on our total being is
much better understood today than formerly, and is
given much more prominence. The value of good and
correct breathing can be seen from those who conduct
ante-natal relaxation courses or take part in various
forms of sport, and also from those who train singers and
musicians.

AWARENESS OF GOD'S PRESENCE

Zen opts for a complete emptying which involves the
complete emptying of oneself and letting go of all ra-
tional thinking, all thoughts, feelings and images. This is
supposed to make one open and receptive to the great
enlightenment. While this method has much to teach us,
nevertheless, for Christians it is probably better to follow

in the footsteps of our own great masters and teachers of prayer.

These great masters constantly draw our attention to the awareness of God's presence. The masters of the past teach us to let go of the external and internal world – to let go of everything and concentrate on the presence of God. The awareness of God's presence is the door to prayer.

You may ask, "Where can I find God – where can I become aware of his presence? Is he outside me or inside me?" God says, "If you seek me you will find me". God is everywhere. We can find him in all that is created. We can find him through our own reflections. We can immerse ourselves completely in a scene from the Gospel and vividly and whole-heartedly live it out, or if we are Catholics and kneel down before the Blessed Sacrament we shall become aware of the Eucharistic presence. If we read his Word in Scripture with faith and love we shall hear his voice. If we are gathered together in his name we shall feel his presence, and if we give a beggar a glass of water we shall see him in the beggar's face. Thus there are many ways and means of becoming aware of God's presence. The best way, however, is to become aware of God's indwelling in us, in our very hearts. St John of the Cross says, "Nowhere will you find God more quickly, more surely and closely, and enjoy his presence more, than in yourself.".

PRAYER TO THE HOLY SPIRIT

We do not know how to pray. We are helpless and all we do or say is so inadequate. Without the Holy Spirit our prayers can hardly be called prayers. So let us come to him at the beginning of all our prayer periods and ask him to lead and guide us. He is the Master of all prayer. Then, if we place ourselves in his hands and make ourselves totally pliable I am quite sure that our prayer will be good and a success, even if we think it is dry, or we are distracted.

I shall now give a few simple and practical exercises. Try to get used to practising one or two of them because in chapters that follow I shall always suggest starting with one or other relaxation exercise before going into prayer.

EXERCISES

No. 1. *Three Deep Breaths*

> Settle comfortably in the position you will hold in prayer . . . take your time . . . move around a few times . . .

> Gently close your eyes . . . do not press them together or keep them tightly shut . . .

> Allow all the air that is in the lungs to seep out, gently contracting the diaphragm (abdomen); do not use force, just sense that you have "emptied out" all the stale air . . .

> Inhale deeply, expanding the diaphragm, and let in a flood of fresh air . . . hold this for a moment – not with discomfort but just to let everything in you be completely still for a few moments and to allow the system to breathe oxygen . . .

> Contract the diaphragm again and allow all the

air to flow out . . .

Do this exercise a few more times.

No. 2. *Breath and Shoulders*

Sit down comfortably . . . close your eyes gently . . . do not keep them tightly shut . . .

Breathe in slowly and deeply, expand the diaphragm and pull your shoulders up as far as you can . . .

Hold your breath and shoulders . . .

Now let your shoulders fall suddenly and let all the air go out with the mouth open . . .

Repeat this a few times.

No. 3. *Rolling the Head*

Sit down comfortably . . . close your eyes gently . . . avoid pressing them together . . .

With your head make as big a circle as possible starting from left to right, slowly – very slowly . . .

Do the same thing starting from right to left . . .

Sit down comfortably . . . close your eyes . . .

Gently expel all the stale air from your lungs by contracting the diaphragm – as you expel the air allow your head to fall down on your chest . . . relax . . .

Now draw-in fresh air and raise your head and let it fall back . . . relax . . .

PART ONE

Repeat this exercise a few times.

Then when inhaling, instead of raising the head and letting it fall back, roll it around to the right until it settles on the back . . . relax . . .

After relaxing . . . exhale and roll the head around till it rests on the chest and all the air is expelled from the lungs . . .

Do this a few times.

No. 4. *Controlled Bodily Relaxation*

Sit down comfortably . . . shift around a few times . . . close your eyes and become still . . .

Focus your attention on your left foot . . . imagine it as being totally relaxed and at ease . . . sense all the tension flowing out of it . . . as the foot is fully relaxed, move on to the ankle . . . again focus your attention on it . . . imagine it fully relaxed . . . all the tension flowing out of it . . .

Move on to the calf . . . and do the same . . . the knee . . . the thigh . . .

Now on to the right foot the ankle . . . calf . . . knee . . . thigh . . .

Now do the hips . . . the stomach, and even its inner organs . . .

Now go to the lower back and move up methodically . . . come to the shoulder blades . . . first the left . . . then the right . . .

Come now to the front . . . the chest . . . left, right

27

. . . the shoulders left, right . . .
Move down the left arm . . . upper arm . . . elbow
. . . forearm . . . hand . . . sense of the tension
flowing out of the tips of the fingers . . .

Now do the right arm . . . upper . . . elbow . . .
forearm . . . hand . . . fingers . . .

Focus your attention on your neck . . . let it relax
all around . . . now the jaws . . . the tongue . . .
the root of the tongue down in the throat . . . all
the muscles around the lips . . . sense the tension
flowing out and everything relaxing . . .

Now take the left cheekbone . . . right cheekbone
. . . the muscles under each eye . . . the eyelids . . .
the eyebrows . . . let the tension flow out of your
furrowed brow and relax – relax – relax . . .

Come to the scalp . . . the skin and muscles in the
back of your head . . . focus your attention on
each area . . . sense the tension flowing out . . .
allow each part to become fully relaxed . . .

No. 5. *Total Relaxation*

Stand up . . . raise your right hand above your head and
reach for the sky . . . really stretch . . . a little more than
you think you can . . . go beyond your limits, just a little
more . . .

Now hold this stretching for a few moments . . .

Now allow the arms to fall gently to the side . . . relax . . .

Next raise your left arm . . . stretch it as far as you can . . .
a little more . . . and still a little more . . . hold it! Let the

arm fall gently to the side . . . relax . . .

Now allow your head to fall forward . . . the arms dangling . . . and the body bending at the waist . . . do not worry about keeping the knees straight . . . be completely relaxed, letting your head fall as far as it will . . . rest in this position . . .

Resume an upright position.

Place your feet together and raise both your arms until they are fully extended, parallel to the shoulders, forming a cross . . . Without moving your feet, gently twist your body to the right as far as you can . . . a little more . . . still a little more . . .

Hold this position for a few moments . . . and straighten up . . .

Now twist as far as you can to the left . . . a little more . . . still more . . . hold it, return to the centre and relax . . . let your arms fall and relax – relax . . .

No. 6. *Breath Counting Exercise*

> a. 1. inhale   – exhale on *one*
>   2. inhale   – exhale on *two*
>   3. inhale   – exhale on *three*
>   4. inhale   – exhale on *four*

> b. Very slowly . . . after you are familiar with the exercise . . . breath through the nostrils . . .

>   1. and inhale   – exhale one
>   2. and inhale   – exhale two
>   3. and inhale   – exhale three
>   4. and inhale   – exhale four

c. 1. inhale Peace   – repeat – exhale – on a person
    2. inhale Love   – repeat – exhale – on a person
    3. inhale Harmony – repeat – exhale – on a person
    4. inhale Freedom – repeat – exhale – on a person

d. Take Freedom, for example:

    1. inhale on 4 counts   freedom for four counts
    2. hold breath   freedom for four counts
    3. exhale 4   freedom for four counts
    4. rest 4   freedom (in our own
                                 freedom space)

Increase to 5 etc . . . very slowly . . . breath deeply
. . . It is the energy of Jesus you are exhaling on
the person . . .

No. 7. *Auto-Suggestive Exercises*

a. Sit down comfortably and relaxed . . . it does
    not matter where . . . it is important that you
    can sit in this position as long as you meditate
    without shifting around . . .

    Now close your eyes and repeat slowly and
    meditatively in your mind the following
    sentences:

    I now have time . . .
    I have ten minutes . . .
    I will not be distracted . . .
    I can be entirely alone . . .
    I am glad to have time . . .
    I am glad to be quiet . . .
    All tensions disappear from me . . .

It becomes very quiet in me . . .
I am quiet . . .
I am quietness . . .
It is very still in me . . .
I am still . . .
I come to myself . . .

b. Once again sit down, comfortable and relaxed
. . . Put your elbows on your knees and put
your head between your hands . . . Close your
eyes . . . now slowly but powerfully with both
hands brush over your face from top to bottom
a few times . . . your elbows remain on your
knees . . . move your head whilst doing this . . .

Now let your left hand rest on your upper leg
and rub your forehead with your right hand
from left to right . . . Do this a few times . . .
Brush once more over your forehead as if you
were brushing away all your sadness . . .

Brush from your forehead over your cheek
until your hand falls off your chin . . . do this a
few times . . .

Take both hands and brush with your finger-
tips, slowly and gently, from the middle of
your forehead over your cheeks down to the
chin . . . the elbows are no longer on your
knees . . .

Sit up slowly . . . lift your face upwards as if
you were looking at the stars, but keep your
eyes closed . . .

Continue the brushing exercises over your

face with your arms and hands . . . always gently and lightly, almost flying over it . . .

Do the forehead – the cheeks – the whole face will relax and lose its tension . . .

Let your hands fall gently on your upper legs and lay them on top of one another like a cup . . .

c. Sit comfortably . . . close your eyes gently and relax . . .

Try to realize the following:

I am now here and have time . . . nothing disturbs me . . . I feel my forehead . . . the tension slowly disappears as if I were to brush it away with a soft cloth . . . no cramps, no wrinkles . . . my forehead is relaxed and free . . .

My eyes are slightly open . . . not pressed together; even my pupils are quiet . . . as if I were looking through closed eyes right at one point before me . . . my eyes are soft and relaxed . . .

My right cheek is relaxed . . . the quiet flows down from my forehead . . . my muscles relax . . . no flickering of nerves . . . the quietness spreads . . .

My lips lie softly on one another . . . my teeth are not pressed together, no tension, no cramp . . . quiet, relaxation and recollection . . . also my tongue lies loose in my mouth . . .

I feel my right arm . . . it hangs lightly from the shoulder, in the joint . . . the muscles are loose, no tension . . . I feel the weight, how the arm hangs in the joint . . . the quiet flows from the forehead over the cheeks into the arm . . . also, the forearm becomes loose, the muscles, sinews and nerves are loose, my arm is totally quiet . . . The quietness flows into the hand . . . the hand is warm, heavy and quiet . . . I feel how the blood flows into the hand . . .

Now do the same over the left side: cheek, arm, hand . . .

Lay your hands on your lap . . . form a cup and feel how the circle is now closed; from the forehead over the arm to the hands – from the hands over the arm to the forehead . . .

By very quiet and relaxed . . .

PART TWO

Praying by simply Being Present

It was a quiet and beautiful afternoon and a woman was kneeling in prayer at the back of the church. Then the door opened to admit two children, a boy and a girl. Having dipped their fingers in the holy water font they made the sign of the cross with great devotion and then proceeded very quietly right to the front of the church, where they sat down in the front bench. The woman in the meantime had been watching very attentively and was greatly delighted with the children's behaviour.

But her delight was soon to turn to disappointment. The children continued sitting, hands in their laps, not even their lips moved. They just sat there, apparently totally inactive. This increased the woman's agitation and nervousness, and although she tried to keep on praying she found it hard to overcome this distraction. Finally she could stand it no longer and approached the children. "But now you must start praying and not just sit there", she told them.

The children replied with a baffled expression on their faces, "But we are praying all the time."

"Which prayers are you saying?" countered the woman.

So surprised were the children at this juncture that they remained silent, not knowing what answer to give as they did not even understand the question.

34

We now have to ask ourselves what "to pray" really means. The short story just related will make us think. Were the children really praying? What form did their prayer take? We can go further, perhaps, and ask if the two questions just raised are justified.

Does prayer always have to take the form of words spoken, and is it always an activity in which the mind is brought into operation? When asked what prayer is, we usually give a twofold answer.:

a. To speak with God.
b. To raise up one's mind and heart to God.

Although these answers are right, we can still ask whether they contain everything that can be said about prayer. Do they exhaust the meaning of the word "prayer", or might we say that they are only two forms of prayer? Must our prayer always involve some kind of activity – a speaking to God – a listening to him – a raising up of the heart?

When we take a good look at the way we spend our lives, we soon realize that in addition to the countless activities in which we partake, there are periods of our lives when we simply "are". We are happy or sad – sure or unsure about things, and so on. There are times, too, when we feel that simply "being" in the company of someone gives us a sense of contentment.

When we apply what has just been said to our relationship with God – being happy in his presence – sure of his protection – being content to be recollected and aware of his presence – isn't that a way of being united with God in prayer? Can't we call all that prayer?

Going back to our opening story, can we not now say that we understand the surprise the children

35

experienced at being questioned? Were they not praying – spending time in God's presence and thereby absorbing something of his peace, his joy and his sense of rest?

There must be many people who would say that prayer surely means much more than just placing oneself in God's presence and doing nothing else. They would argue:

a. Hasn't God given us a mind with which we should think and reflect on him, and a tongue with which to talk to him and to give him praise and thanks.
b. Have we not got to be active in putting our talents to use?

Is there anything meaningful in just sitting doing nothing – in just being there? Again, many people would ask what would be the value of prayer if we just sit with our hands in our lap doing absolutely nothing. Don't we often hear it said "Don't come before the Lord with empty hands"?

These and similar objections could be raised and there is some truth in them. It cannot be denied that God has given us a mind which we should use to think of him and reflect on him. But the question can be asked "Have we always got to use our mind in prayer?" We can go further and ask if it is not also a sign of honour and respect towards God if now and then we stop all our thinking and reflection, and instead allow ourselves to become aware of his presence, realizing that he will always remain "unknowable" and that we will never be able to understand him fully with our limited powers of mind.

The same can be said about our lips. Have we got to be praising and thanking him all the time with words? To become aware of God's presence in silence, in the knowledge that whatever we say we will never be able to praise and thank him adequately, is that not a good and meaningful form of prayer?

The same thing can be applied to our activities. Does God want to see us *doing* something every time we pray? Is there no place for *rest* in prayer?

When the disciples returned from their first mission and told Jesus of all the successes they had achieved in his name, he did not say to them "Well done". Nor did he continue by telling them that they had worked and done so much for others and that it was now time for them to do something for God. All he said was "Come away by yourselves to a lonely place and rest for a while" (Mark 6:31).

On another occasion Jesus spoke to people carrying heavy responsibilities, and who doubtless were worried over all sorts of human problems. He did not tell them "Come and join me in my work". All he said was "Come to me and take your rest" (Matthew 11:28).

So, if now and then when engaged in prayer, we neither speak, listen nor think about God, are we not doing the very thing he wants – just "being" with him?

God himself is constantly at work keeping the universe in existence. It is said that on the seventh day he rested (Genesis 2:2). This means that not only is God eternally active but he is also the great and eternal Rest. The Letter to the Hebrews encourages us to try to enter into this Rest of God: "Let us also strive to enter into God's sabbath rest" (4:11). We find the same idea in St Bonaventure's writings. In his book *The Ascent of Man to God* he relates how man climbs up the six-step ladder to the throne of God where all activity ceases and the pray-er no longer does anything but rest in the great peace of God. There can be many and various occasions in our life when we can practise this simple form of prayer. All we have to do is to sit down, place our hands in our lap, give up all thinking and reflecting as far as possible, let go of all feelings and emotions and simply occupy ourselves with the idea "I just want to be here before God" – simply to be with him – just to be in his presence. All that I need do is simply say in my mind "I just want to be here with you, O Lord".

We will, of course, frequently fail in our efforts "just to be", so prone are we to distractions. Yet we should not be deterred, but simply, in great calm and patience, come back to the thought "I just want to be here with you, O my Lord". We will find that all sorts of worries, problems, desires and longings intrude. As we become aware of these we can say, "With all my problems, worries, desires and longings I am here with you, O Lord". We will want to praise and thank the Lord for being allowed simply to be in his presence, but let us not be in a hurry to do so. We should take our time, just being there with him for whom our heart longs and whom we love. Just be there and don't worry about anything else.

Even when taking a stroll or when at work, we can reassure ourselves with the thought that we are always and everywhere in God's presence. It is simply a matter of continually reminding ourselves "I am here with you, O my Lord".

The words " I am here" are few, yet they are very important. They play an important part in our daily life as well as in Scripture. When a child is born it announces its arrival to all with its first cry: "I am here". It is the same in the typical home. The husband comes in from work,

38

takes off his hat and coat and calls, "Are you in, dear?" The wife answers, "Yes I am here". It may seem all very common-place but for two people who love each other, this exchange of greetings means a great deal.

We find this same idea in the Bible. In the book of Baruch 3:35 we read, "When he calls the stars they answer: 'Here we are'." Again, in the book of Job (38;35) we find, "You send forth the lightnings and they say: 'Here we are'." In Genesis it is related how God wanted to test Abraham with a command to sacrifice his son, Isaac. The story begins with God calling Abraham by name. He answers, "Yes, here I am". Similarly on two occasions Jacob answered, "Yes, here I am" when God called him (Genesis 31:11, 24;2).

The same thing happened when God revealed himself to Moses in the burning bush. Again, who does not know of the threefold "Here I am" of the young Samuel as God called him by name in the middle of the night? (1 Samuel 3:4).

Much later, as the Church developed her services, these few words acquired the notion of giving consent to God's calling. In the ordination to the priesthood and in the profession of monks and nuns, at a certain stage in the ceremony the candidate is addressed by name. The candidate then comes forward to the bishop or superior and says, "Here I am".

These few instances show us the meaning of simply being present before God. They show also how these simple words can express our love for God and our readiness just to be present with him without words or actions coming into play.

A Loving Person

— Find a comfortable posture . . . close your eyes . . . and quieten yourself . . .

— Do one of the relaxation exercises . . .

— Take two or three deep breaths . . . then let your breathing return to its normal rhythm . . . be aware of it without controlling it . . . then forget it . . .

— Ask the Holy Spirit to guide you through this prayer . . .

— Think of a person who loves you very much, and is very close to you . . . If you want to show him your affection, your gratitude and love . . . you don't need to prove that to him . . . Just to be with him is quite enough . . . It tells him that you love him . . .

— Think of Jesus as this person who loves you so much . . . you want to show to him that you love him too . . . Show that to him by just wanting to be with him . . . "Lord I just want to be with you because I love you" . . . Stay all the time with this thought . . . when you get off the track . . . just come back again and keep on repeating: "Lord, I want to be with you because I love you." Spend all the time with this thought . . . Do nothing else . . .

— When you feel the time is right, begin to close your prayer and thank God . . .

— Slowly and gently open your eyes and end the prayer.

Jesus and Mary

— Find a comfortable posture . . . close your eyes . . . and quieten yourself . . .

— Do one of the relaxation exercises . . .

— Take two or three deep breaths . . . then let your breathing return to its normal rhythm . . . Be aware of it without controlling it . . . then let it go . . .

— Ask the Holy Spirit to guide you through this prayer . . .

— Place yourself in the house of Martha and Mary of Bethany . . . See Mary sitting at the feet of Jesus . . . Jesus probably did not speak all the time nor did Mary listen all the time . . . there were surely periods when both were silent . . . Imagine this scene and place yourself in it . . . Sit at the feet of your beloved master . . . just enjoy sitting there . . . give up all Martha's jobs and just spend the time with your Lord doing nothing, saying nothing . . . Just be there with the idea of enjoying your Master . . . whenever you get distracted gently come back again to this idea . . .

— When you feel the time is right, begin to close your prayer and thank God . . .

— Slowly and gently open your eyes and end the prayer.

Here I Am

— Find a comfortable posture . . . close your eyes . . . and quieten yourself . . .

— Do one of the relaxation exercises . . .

— Take two or three deep breaths . . . then let the breathing become normal again . . . do not control it . . . just become aware of it . . . then let it go . . .

— Ask the Holy Spirit to guide you through this prayer . . .

— Imagine one of these scenes: God calling Abraham, or Moses before the burning bush, or the young Samuel being called by God at night . . . Imagine this scene as vividly as possible – live yourself into it . . .

— Hear God calling them and hear them answering: "Here I am." Listen attentively to the answer: "Here I am." . . .

— Put yourself there – hear God calling your name, then answer him "Here I am." put your whole self into the words. Be aware of God and of your saying "Here I am". Whenever you get distracted say again a few time "Here I am" and then just rest in the awareness . . .

Hannah
Mary

— When you feel the time is right, begin to close your prayer and thank God . . .

— Slowly and gently open your eyes and end the prayer.

42

The Silent Forest

— Find a comfortable posture . . . close your eyes . . . and
  quieten yourself . . .

— Do one of the relaxation exercises . . .

— Take two or three deep breaths . . . then let your
  breathing return to its normal rhythm . . . be aware of
  your breathing without controlling it . . . then forget it
  . . .

— Ask the Holy Spirit to guide you through this prayer
  . . .

— I want you to think of a forest covered in snow or white
  frost . . . Nothing moves . . . all is still . . . nothing is
  happening . . . the forest is simply there . . . it simply *is*
  . . . for the glory of God.

— I want you to go into this forest . . . Imagine yourself to
  be there . . . Become aware of the stillness . . . peace
  . . . and quiet. Just let all this quiet and peace enter you
  . . . saturate yourself with it . . . but do nothing . . .
  You are just there . . .

— Say to Our Lord: "Like this forest I just like to be here
  before you, O my Lord." Do nothing else . . . Don't
  worry about distractions . . . Just keep on saying from
  time to time: "I just want to be here with you, O my
  Lord". . . .

— When you feel the time is right, begin to close your
  prayer and thank God . . . Slowly and gently open
  your eyes and end the prayer.

The Starry Sky

— Find a comfortable posture . . . close your eyes . . . and quieten yourself . . .

— Do one of the relaxation exercises . . .

— Take two or three deep breaths . . . then let it become normal again . . . do not control it . . . just become aware of it . . . then let it go . . .

— Ask the Holy Spirit to guide you through this prayer . . .

— I want you to imagine a clear winter's night . . . look up into the sky and see the billions of stars . . . you probably know only a few of them . . . Why are they there? . . . Simply to be a luminous hymn of praise to the Creator . . .

— Let the beauty and marvel, the praise and glory of these billions of stars enter deep into you . . .

— Say to our Lord: "As the millions of stars in the sky give praise and glory to you by just being there, so I want to give you praise and glory by just being here in your presence" . . . Don't do anything else . . . Your very being there in the presence of God is glory and praise enough . . . When distracted just come back again to being present to the Lord . . .

— When you feel the time is right, begin to close your prayer and thank God . . .

— Slowly and gently open your eyes and end the prayer.

Resting with Jesus

- Find a comfortable posture . . . close your eyes . . . and quieten yourself . . .

- Do one of the relaxation exercises . . .

- Take two or three deep breaths . . . then let the breathing become normal again . . . do not control it . . . just become aware of it . . . then let it go . . .

- Ask the Holy Spirit to guide you through this prayer . . .

- When the Apostles told Jesus all they had done, he told them, "Come with me to a lonely place and rest for a while" . . .

- Imagine the Disciples with Jesus in a lonely place . . . they rest and relax with him . . . Perhaps they sit or lie down . . . fully resting and relaxing in his presence . . .

- Here Jesus saying to you "Come to me and rest for a while" . . . Hear these words over and over again . . .

- Go to him and relax . . . don't do anything . . . don't tell him all your problems . . . don't ask him all kinds of questions . . . just rest . . . with him, in his company . . . bathe yourself in his presence . . . You may lay your head on his chest if you want or hold his hand and be at peace, and rest, and rest . . . If you get distracted listen to the words again; "Come to me and rest for a while" . . .

- When you feel the time is right, begin to close your prayer and thank God . . .

- Slowly and gently open your eyes and end the prayer.

45

PART THREE

Praying in harmony with Breathing

At first breathing appears to be a purely physical process. We inhale clean, fresh air and breathe out air carrying impurities of various sorts. This seems to be all that there is to breathing – keeping us alive. When we no longer breathe, we die.

We may well ask what breathing has to do with prayer, in the light of what has just been said. From the physical point of view, breathing is the most basic sign of life, but though it *is* one of its most essential activities it is one of the least recognized and reflected on. As children, we saw our breath in the wintry weather when we breathed out into the frosty air. When learning to swim we had to learn to hold our breath under the water. When running, or playing strenuously, we get out of breath.

We know what happens when we get angry. People will tell us to cool down, and the taking of a few deep breaths will help to ease the anger in us. So we can see that there is some kind of connection between our breathing and our feelings and emotions. Our breathing is like a barometer of our feelings. When we are anxious or excited, our breathing becomes agitated, but when the anxiety and excitement pass, our breathing becomes calm once more. In sleep, or during periods of relaxation, our breathing is steady, but when we are suddenly confronted by danger we breathe very rapidly, and sometimes hold our breath.

After the danger has passed, we breathe a sigh of relief and normal breathing takes place once more.

These few examples show us quiet clearly that there is a connection – an interaction – between our breathing and our feelings and emotions. Our feelings and emotions can influence our breathing, and our breathing can influence our feelings and emotions – in our breathing the whole person is involved.

But we may still ask: What has all that to do with prayer? If we turn to the Bible we will see definite connections. In the Bible we see that breathing, especially in the form of "breath" itself, is an image of God's activity. In Genesis 2:7 we read: "Then the Lord God formed man of dust from the ground, and breathed into his nostrils the breath of life."

The prophet Ezekiel saw in his vision a great number of dead bones. He received an order from God to prophesy over them: "Come from the four winds, O breath, and breathe upon these slain, that they may live" (37:1).

Sighing is a form of breathing, and in that light we can think of St Paul's words in the letter to the Romans: "We do not know how to pray as we ought, but the Spirit himself intercedes for us with sighs too deep for words" (8:26).

Our bodily breathing understood as "breath" and as "sighing" is therefore an image of a religious action. As the stretching out of our arms is a sign of bringing our petitions before God, and as kneeling with our hands together we express our adoration of God, so our breathing can be used in prayer to help us grow closer to God.

Breathing has always played an important part in the Christian tradition of prayer. The best-known example is the Jesus Prayer: "Lord Jesus Christ, Son of God, have mercy on me, a sinner." Even in the early days of the Church, monks would give guidance on how to breathe while saying that prayer.

There is, however, an even earlier prayer form known as the "Sigh". This aims at establishing a connection between our breathing and what is taking place in our hearts – sorrow over our sins – the awareness of our miserable situation at our sufferings and the desire to be redeemed from them by God. We can find many psalms and sayings in the Bible that express this relationship between the inner longing of the heart and the outer expression in "sighing".

People may think that a sigh is associated with something tragic or something to be avoided – a sign of weakness even. But when we ponder St Hildegard's words we will see that sighing, for her, meant something totally different. For her it involved a deep longing for union with God, a longing filled with power and expectation.

So breathing has its own rhythm – and is a pointer to the different and difficult feelings and emotions we experience. But it also plays a part in our more positive experiences. When we stand in front of something beautiful we hold our breath, or take a deep breath, which expresses our sense of wonder. In this way, we are expressing physically what we are experiencing in our spirit: we are taking into our heart something beautiful, and trying to keep it there for some time. When we breathe out again, this same sense finds expression in our breathing. The pause at the end of an out-breath is a moment of stillness, of silence, a confident waiting for the next breath in.

It is important to keep this connection in mind when we choose our prayer words or phrases and it is what is meant by praying in unison with our breathing.

There are, of course, a few difficulties which we may all experience with this form of prayer. All I can do is entreat you not to be put off by them! Some of the difficulties may be of a very personal nature, and so may be better dealt with by each person individually, perhaps with the help of a trusted guide or friend.

In a general way though, the first, and perhaps greatest, difficulty for many people is that they do not breathe correctly. They breathe far too quickly. Even a short "One-Word-Prayer" is still too long for them as they cannot fit it in. So the first point to be made is that nothing at all need be done or achieved. We should just repeat the "One-Word-Prayer" in a quiet and relaxed and rhythmic manner, paying no attention to our breathing, but trying to enter more and more deeply into the meaning and sense of the prayer. When we pay sufficient attention to this, we will find that our breathing has adjusted itself to the rhythm of the words prayed.

The reason for our faulty, quick breathing lies in the fact that we are often so harassed, so tense, and so full of nervous energy in our daily lives. It is, therefore, to our own benefit to learn to quieten down and relax, perhaps to live a simpler life in whatever way we can. A lot of Asian forms of meditation can help here such as Transcendental Meditation and Yoga.

One method of relaxing, amongst many others, is known as Autogenic training. We may not be able to follow an actual course but we might make use of the following simple procedure.

49

Take some time off to relax by doing absolutely nothing. Sit down in comfort, place your hands in your lap and just listen to your breathing, and under no circumstances try consciously to control your breathing to make it slow down. You will then notice that it will gradually and quite automatically slow itself down and become quieter. The emphasis should be on the slow out-breath and the little pause at the end.

Another method of relaxation involves the practice of sighing. We have many reasons for sighing and we should do so wordlessly. Just keep on sighing. In due course we will find that the breathing has become quieter and that it is now possible to fit in a "One-Word-Prayer" – perhaps in breathing in, "I am full of tensions" and in breathing out, "I lay them all in your hands, O Lord".

A further difficulty people experience is that though everything outwardly appears in order, we *feel* nothing. We say the words in harmony with our breathing, but we do not feel anything. We are not moved, in spite of all that we have done. This difficulty is very normal in this kind of prayer, so please try not to let it worry you, though I know that is easier said than done!

The problem may lie in the fact that thinking and reflecting on something is easy and can be done quickly enough, but until our heart and emotions are aroused by the word, *time* must pass, with the patient repetition of the "One-Word-Prayer" over and over again. We should repeat the prayer with every breath for 15–20 minutes and longer if necessary. We may have to do this for days, even months, until what has previously been only no-tional will shift from the mind to our feelings and emotions.

Another difficulty may arise for some of us. The prayer word chosen might not move us, but leave us cold, because it does not correspond to the emotional state in which we find ourselves at the time. Then we may have to listen to ourselves and find out which of the many "One-Word-Prayers" will fit our state of mind at that moment.

All our efforts can only be a preparation for what God wants to do in us. Sometimes he will touch us very deeply and rouse our emotions and at other times not. All this we have to leave to him in great humility and try not to worry or become discouraged. What we *can* do is simply to hand ourselves over to the Spirit of God through the exercise of a "One-Word-Prayer" or any other contemplative prayer, so that he may act in us with "sighs" and "prayers" which we ourselves are unable to express by our own efforts.

Awareness of your breathing

In all forms of Oriental meditation, breathing is very important. Western medical opinion agrees that deep abdominal breathing is health-giving and invigorating. Insights from the Orient reinforce this understanding, namely that the breath or the air is the main source of life. This is variously described as "Prana", "Chi" or "Cosmic Energy".

"The wise man breathes from his heels", says an old Chinese proverb. This refers to the awareness of the breath or "Chi", which flows through the body in this kind of meditation. Another Oriental master says, "Your breathing is your greatest friend. Return to it in all your troubles and you will find comfort and guidance."

— Become aware of your breathing . . . just the fact that you are breathing . . . just observe how you are breathing . . .

— Become aware of the air as it comes in and goes out through your nostrils . . . in what part you feel the touch of the air when you inhale . . . and in what part when you exhale . . .

— Become aware, if you can, even of the warmth and coldness of the air, the coolness when you inhale and the warmth when you exhale . . .

— You may also become aware that the quantity of air that passes through one nostril is greater than the amount that passes through the other . . .

— Be sensitive and alert to the slightest and lightest touch of the air as you inhale and exhale . . . keep on doing this for some time, just trying to pick up all the sensations of your breathing that you can . . . whenever you get distracted, just gently and calmly return to the awareness of your sensations . . .

— After some time you may come to great peace and calmness. If you do, just rest in it . . .

— Slowly and gently open your eyes and end your silent prayer . . .

Breathing in God's Breath and Breathing out all Negativeness

God is in all things and all things are in God. He creates,

indwells and works in all things. All things are charged with God's power, God's Spirit, God's life-giving breath. So if we breathe in air we can become aware that we are breathing in God's life-giving spirit. We are breathing in God. This activity can become a beautiful prayer if we breathe in, in order to take in God, to be filled by him, to be transformed by him, but in our breathing out we must then let go of all negativeness. All that is not from God, that is not filled with God's Spirit, we breathe out. I have personally discovered that this is a most wonderful prayer. I have suggested it to many retreatants who have found it very helpful. I also find it very helpful for "asking" prayers, in praying for peace and well-being in the world.

— Find a comfortable posture . . . close your eyes . . . and quieten yourself . . .

— Do one of the relaxation exercises . . .

— Become aware of the Holy Spirit living in you . . . ask him to pray in you . . .

— Become aware of your breathing . . . notice all the sensations in the nostrils . . . watch the air going in and out . . . While you breathe in, be aware . . . fill your lungs with the energy that the Spirit brings . . . While you breathe out, imagine you are breathing out all your impurities . . . your fears . . . your negative feelings . . . your sins . . .

— Stay with this awareness of breathing *in* the breath of God, and breathing *out* all your negativeness . . . Just be aware of this breathing in and breathing out . . .

— Imagine you see your whole body become radiant and alive through this process of breathing in God's life-giving Spirit and breathing out all your negativeness . . .

— Imagine you are stretching out your hands and God's energy, his power, his peace and his Spirit flow out into the world . . .

— Slowly and gently open your eyes and end the prayer.

Breathing in God

How quickly we become aware of city air in contrast to country air; the light air of the mountains, the heavy air of the sea; the tired air of night, the fresh air of morning. The bracing air of May, the sharp, chill, piercing air of December. "The wind blows wherever it pleases. We hear its sound but we cannot tell where it comes from nor where it is going. That is how it is with all who are born of the Spirit" (John 3:8). The winter and spring winds are a child's first experience of mystery, of a transcendence beyond his vocabulary and beyond that of his parents.

Who can tame the wind? Wind overpowers the voices of men and commands their silence. The wind is the breath of God's power and compels our reverence. What is more powerful than a hurricane or a tornado sweeping up everything in its path? What is more gentle than the caress of a spring breeze? Such is our God.

The air is universal and common to us all! We share it with all that has life – people, animals, trees, vegetation, mountains, the earth itself. Into this common air Jesus

54

came. He breathed our breath. And now we breathe his breath, not merely the breath of the lungs, but the breath of the Spirit. In giving us his Spirit, he has breathed into us eternal breath. The breath he gives is his risen life. As the "last Adam" Jesus in his Resurrection becomes the living Spirit.

And so all life, all holiness comes from God through his son Jesus Christ our Lord, by the working of the Holy Spirit.

— Find a comfortable posture . . . close your eyes . . . and quieten yourself . . .

— Do one of the relaxation exercises . . .

— Become aware of the Holy Spirit living in you . . . ask him to pray in you . . .

— Become aware of your breathing . . . try to pick up all the sensations that you feel in your nostrils as you breathe . . . become aware of the air passing through your nostrils, in and out . . . just notice all these things . . . be fully alert and aware . . .

— Now try to reflect on the fact that the air you are breathing in is charged with the power and presence of God . . . think of it as an immense ocean that surrounds you . . . an ocean heavily coloured with God's presence and God's being . . . While you are drawing the air into your lungs you are drawing in God . . . Let every breath you take be a deep sigh of longing for God. Become aware of your drawing in his power and presence of God each time you breathe in . . . stay with this awareness as long as you can . . . If you become distracted go back to the awareness of your breathing in your nostrils . . .

— Slowly and gently open your eyes and end the prayer.

The Liberating Sigh

We often feel annoyed with people or even with ourselves. We may feel depressed, dissatisfied or experience a mood of despair. Perhaps we may be troubled by feelings of guilt which we are unable to get rid of. We may be tormented to death by one or other fear. In short there are *many* states of mind to which we are prone which we cannot just drive away. What *can* we do?

The first step towards liberating ourselves is to admit and accept that we *are* angry, agitated, depressed, full of fear and so on. Probably we will admit to these dispositions only notionally but that is not sufficient. We must really *feel* the fear, the loneliness, and whatever else bothers us, physically. Once we succeed in doing that then it will be natural for us to breathe a deep sigh of relief, and as we do so some of the fear, loneliness and any other negative dispositions we have will flow out with our sigh. That is why we call this process the "liberating sigh" as it relieves our tensions, and helps us to relax and in this way when we do this in God's presence it becomes a prayer. If we can imagine ourselves in the breathing in as the poor, miserable creature that we are, unable to liberate ourselves from our aversions towards others, from internal restlessness, from our feelings of fear and guilt, then as we breathe out we will with all confidence place our problems and worries, and all that burden us, into the hands of our living Father. There is nothing to prevent us from using this "liberating sigh" over and over again. We simply sit down for a while using this form of prayer in the presence of God and arise feeling refreshed and light of heart.

- Find a comfortable posture . . . close your eyes . . . and quieten yourself . . .

- Do one of the relaxation exercises . . .

- Become aware of the Holy Spirit living in you . . . ask him to pray in you . . .

- Become aware of your breathing . . . notice sensations in the nostrils . . . watch the air going in and out . . .

- While you breathe in, become aware of your poverty, misery and sinfulness and whatever other difficult feelings are bothering you, and how you are unable to help yourself . . . Fill your lungs with the breath of God . . . He will free you . . . and while you breathe out imagine you are breathing out all your impurities, fears and negative feelings . . .

- Stay with this activity of breathing in and out all the time during your prayer . . . when breathing in be aware of your poverty . . . when breathing out put all your problems and worries into the hands of the Lord as he stands before you . . .

- Slowly and gently open your eyes and end the prayer.

Father into your Hands

According to St Luke 23:46 Jesus's last words were a trustful: "Father, into your hands I commend my spirit." We can use these same words as a form of praying the "liberating sigh". With us the word "Father" would not contain the same force or pathos as when Christ uttered that word. It could not well up and burst forth from our heart with the same trust and confidence as in the case of Jesus. But we can unite ourselves with Jesus and pray with him: "Father, into your hands I comment my spirit", and as we breathe out, our misery and fear will ebb away and be replaced with our trust and confidence, which we will pour out into the hands of our loving Father.

Christ, in his last hour, used the "liberating sigh" as a prayer, and we can follow his example by making this prayer our own, so that we may find peace, rest and security in the hands of our loving and compassionate father.

— Find a comfortable posture . . . close your eyes . . . and quieten yourself . . .

— Do one of the relaxation exercises . . .

— Become aware that you are here to pray . . . ask the Holy Spirit living in you to pray in you . . .

— Become aware of your breathing . . . observe your breathing in and out . . . watch all the sensations . . .

— Now I want you to become aware of God, our loving and merciful Father . . . Cry out to him, "Father into your hands I commend my spirit" . . . As you breathe in concentrate on the Father, and as you breathe out

58

put all your fears and misery and problems with confidence into his loving hands . . . You need not say words . . . but be aware of what you are doing with each breath . . . Keep on focusing on your breath and what you want to express by it . . . Do not give up . . .

– Slowly and gently open your eyes and end the prayer.

We – You

A mother of several children found that for her the best prayer was "We – You". She used this for all her needs. When troubled with worries or problems concerning her children, in her imagination she would take them in her arms and pray this prayer with them. She did the same when full of joy, thanking God with all her children. Because she was present to God with her children in this prayer, she experienced not only her oneness with God but also her oneness with her children in a new and much deeper way.

Many similar experiences are enjoyed by married couples and young lovers who pray in this way. They discover a much deeper meaning in their love. Many of us are put off with all the misery and suffering in today's world. By bringing all of it to mind, and including all who suffer as a result, we can take it into the "We" of our prayer, and then in the "You" come before God, asking and trusting in his goodness.

We can also embrace in our "We" all that we see and hear, indeed, the whole of God's creation, and then make our "You" into a great song celebrating all that God has created. Gradually we will become aware that our prayer is no longer just something of the mind. It becomes more all-embracing. It will embrace our whole being as we stand in God's presence and are drawn towards him. In this prayer we give to our "I" a direction, a meaning, a purpose, a God: the "You" of God.

— Find a comfortable posture . . . close your eyes . . . and quieten yourself . . .

— Do one of the relaxation exercises . . .

— Become consciously aware that you are here to pray . . . ask the Holy Spirit to pray in you . . .

— Become aware of your breathing . . . observe the rhythm of your breathing . . .

— Gather around you your family, or your friends, or your community, or whomever you want to pray for: take them under your arms and go to the Lord . . . Stand before the Lord and just say, or rather be aware of, the "We" as you breathe in the "You" (God) as you breathe out . . . "We – You" . . . Keep on doing this . . . Do not think or keep your gaze on the "we", whoever they are, but concentrate on the "We – You" as you breathe in and out . . . be aware of the breathing . . .

— Slowly and gently open your eyes and end the prayer.

To receive in order to give

When we breathe in, we receive or take in something, in order to give it away again in our breathing out. Let us look at our human existence. All that we have and all we have received – life from our parents, our upbringing and education from parents, teachers and the Church. Our encounters with people of all sorts enrich us spiritually and psychologically. Our whole existence consists in the fact that we are receivers.

The same is true of our Christian existence: we have received the sacraments, they are all gifts from God. We are always the ones who receive, we are the containers . . . All the gifts, talents and graces received impose certain duties on us. We have received all that we have been given so that we can give them back to our Lord in praise and thanksgiving, in the first instance, and secondly so that we can use them in the service of our brothers and sisters. We must not bury our talents or let them lie unused. We have received them so that we can give them away.

Now it is precisely this human and Christian existence of ours that is reflected in our breathing in and out. We take in something to ourselves in order to give it away again. So we can in all stillness listen to our breathing, and as we take each breath say, "I receive", while saying as we breathe out, "In order to give". By doing this we will experience that our whole existence is being receivers in order to become givers.

– Find a comfortable posture . . . close your eyes . . . and quieten yourself . . .

– Do one of the relaxation exercises . . .

– Become consciously aware of your breathing . . . watch it as you breathe in and out . . .

– Become aware of some of the things that you have received – from people . . . from God . . .

– Notice that you have received them not to store them up or to bury them . . . but to give them back to God, the giver, or to hand them on to others . . .

– As you breathe in be aware that you constantly receive . . . in your breathing out be aware that you receive in order to give . . . Keep concentrating on your breathing, aware that you receive in order to give . . . Relax . . . just watch as you breathe in and out and be aware of what you want to express by it: that you receive . . . in order to give . . .

– Slowly and gently open your eyes and end the prayer.

"All evil away from me Lord Jesus rule you in me"

There are many therapists and breath experts who say that we should always begin with the breathing out. When we fully exhale, then breathing in will come naturally. A great number of "Gurus" and teachers of Asian methods of meditation subscribe to the same view. One thing is certain: that if we want to be filled by God, then we must first of all present ourselves before him as empty vessels. So we must let go of all the tensions, fears, anxieties in us, every time we breathe out. Are not the tensions in us sometimes indications that we hold on to, and are often enslaved by, things that hinder us from being free for God? We must therefore, in our breathing out, literally, put off the old man – let him go – let him come out of us – so that in breathing in, we can become new persons. So in breathing out we try to let go of everything that hinders us from being free for God, so that in breathing in we can let ourselves be filled with God's rest, peace, greatness, power, or whatever other concept we have of God. There are plenty of short prayer words suitable for this kind of prayer that blend with our breathing. There is, for instance, a little prayer for children that could be used, "All evil away from me – Lord Jesus rule you in me".

– Find a comfortable posture . . . close your eyes . . . and quieten yourself . . .

– Do one of the relaxation exercises

– Be consciously aware that you are here to pray . . .

– Ask the Holy Spirit to guide you . . .

– Now become aware of the possible negativeness, tension and lack of freedom in you . . . perhaps there is some particular thing that blocks you . . . that holds you tight . . . Now long to be free from all these bonds . . . decide to let go . . . to empty yourself of all that is negative so that you can be filled with God, his peace, his love . . .

– Express this longing in your breathing . . . As you breathe out let go of all that is evil: "All evil away from me", and as you breathe in be filled with God, his peace, his power: "Lord Jesus rule you in me".

  Just concentrate on your breathing out – in, out – in; through this you express bodily what you desire in your heart . . .

– Slowly and gently open your eyes and end the prayer.

Dying and rising

Much has been written, and a great deal of thought expended, on the text of Romans 6:3, and there is still no end to the writings and discussions about it. We might come to a quicker and deeper understanding of this text by praying and contemplating it. We must take the main idea of the text and then let the Spirit take over. We become aware of the word **dying** when breathing out, and of the word **rising** when breathing in. Of course at first we will think and reflect on what **dying** means to us: dying to self, dying to all that hinders us from being free for God, from all self-centredness. The same will hold good for the word **rising.** What does it mean to us? It means power, strength, glory and a totally new life. In this form of prayer we can almost experience physically and spiritually how this new life, this power, this glory of God flows into us.

– Find a comfortable posture . . . close your eyes . . . and quieten yourself . . .

– Do one of the relaxation exercises . . .

– Become aware that you are here to pray and ask the Holy Spirit living in you to pray in you and lead and guide you . . .

– St Paul Romans 6:3 says: "Do you know that all of us who have been baptized into Christ were baptized into his death? We were buried therefore with him by baptism into death, so that, as Christ was raised from the dead by the glory of the Father, we too walk in newness of life. For if we have been united with him in a death like his, we shall certainly be united with him in a resurrection like his."

– Become aware of your breathing . . . watch your breathing in and out . . . notice all the little sensations . . .

– Take up St Paul's thoughts on dying and rising. And while you breathe out think of dying . . . at the beginning you may want to reflect on what this dying means for you . . . Dying to all that hinders you on the way to God . . . but do not use your mind too much . . . just keep thinking of dying while breathing out – and while you breathe in think of rising. Rising can mean much . . . it promises a new life . . . a totally new life . . . just be aware of the rising as you breathe in and feel in your body how this new life, power and glory of God flows in to you as you breathe in . . .

– Slowly and gently open your eyes and end the prayer.

PART FOUR

Praying with One Word

The first Christian monks in the third century lived as hermits in the desert, south of the Nile Delta and became known as "The Desert Fathers". From time to time young applicants presented themselves to learn from them and become their pupils. These young men looked on the monks as their Fathers and called them "Abba", as they were wise, old and saintly, and near to God.

One day a young monk came to Abba Peter and asked him: "What must I do, to pray well?" The Abba answered: "You have a book of the psalms, haven't you? You know many of them. Is there any particular psalm that you like very much? One that you like to pray?"

The young man answered: "Yes, Father, I have such a psalm." Abba Peter went on: "And is there perhaps in this psalm a verse that you particularly like, one that especially appeals to you?" "Yes, indeed", was the reply. "Very well, then, use that verse as your prayer." "This verse I will have said in no time. What then?", asked the young man. Abba Peter replied: "Use that verse as your prayer for an hour and then come back to me."

Not surprisingly the young monk was very puzzled at this but he consoled himself with the thought, "I shall try to do what I have been told." Off he went and did what he had been told to do. After an hour he returned and reported to Abba Peter, "I have prayed for a full hour using that verse as my prayer. What next?" Abba Peter said: "Continue to use that verse as your prayer." "But for how long?" asked the young man. "Use it as your prayer for the whole of today and come back tomorrow."

At this stage the young monk was lost for words, so great was his astonishment, but as he had made up his mind to take Abba Peter for his spiritual guide, he complied, even though he could not help feeling that the advice he had been given was practically meaningless.

The following day he came back and reported that he had used that single verse as a prayer over and over again for the whole day. "What must I do now?" he enquired. Abba Peter smiled at him and said: "Use that verse as your prayer." Once more the young man asked, "For how long?" "A whole week, then come back again", was the reply.

Our young monk forced himself to use that one verse as his prayer not only for a whole day but for the whole week, after which he returned to Abba Peter. This time he pleaded with him: "May I keep this one verse as my prayer?" Abba Peter nodded knowingly and said: "If you want to pray well it will be sufficient for you to use that verse as your prayer over and over again for the rest of your life."

This story brings out some important truths.

Firstly: a method of prayer which involves repeating again and again a short sentence, or a word, from Scripture or some other book on spirituality, is an exceedingly old tradition in the Church. We know that some men and women, far back in history, did in fact spend their entire lives using the "One-Word-Prayer", as it was called.

Secondly: this story shows that, at first, such a form of praying seems meaningless, almost foolish. One has to discipline oneself with great determination to turn back to this one thought, or word, when difficulties are experienced. If we manage to do this we may begin to enjoy this form of prayer; we may realize that it is in fact full of meaning and one that continually enlightens, and sinks more and more into our being.

Thirdly: the "One-Word-Prayer" is a form of praying that can lead us on to tremendous heights and depths of experience in our spiritual lives.

This prayer can led us to a special kind of tranquillity as our concentration on the Word or Phrase gradually helps to control our wandering thoughts.

This sense of peace will slowly permeate our other senses – and little by little our whole inner self will be at peace. But don't worry if you do not experience the peace instantly. The aim of this prayer is not to achieve peace. It is a prayer, and peace is only one effect. The peace will come gradually but surely.

You are my delight and my joy

– Find a comfortable posture . . . close your eyes . . . and quieten yourself . . .

– Do one of the relaxation exercises . . .

– Take two or three deep breaths . . . then let your breathing return to its normal rhythm . . . be aware of

your breathing without controlling it . . . then forget it
. . .

- Ask the Holy Spirit to guide you through this prayer
  . . .

- Think of a situation in your life in which you experienced great joy . . . Relive the situation again . . .

- Imagine the Lord is also present . . . He is so delighted
  . . . His whole being radiates joy . . .

- The Lord comes to you and says: "You are my delight
  and joy . . . You are my greatest joy, you are my
  everything, I love you so much" . . . Hear these words
  being said to you again and again . . . say them to
  yourself . . . make little pauses to allow the full meaning to seep into your heart and touch you . . . try not to
  allow your mind to wander, just try to stay with this one
  Word: "X, you are my delight and my joy" . . . Keep
  focusing on this and this alone . . . just let these words
  sink deep into you . . .

- When you feel the time is right, begin to close your
  prayer and thank God. . .

- Slowly and gently open your eyes and end the prayer.

Lord, I believe, help my unbelief

- Find a comfortable posture . . . close your eyes . . . and
  quieten yourself . . .

- Do one of the relaxation exercises . . .

— Take two or three deep breaths . . . then let your breathing return to its normal rhythm . . . be aware of it without controlling it . . . then forget it . . .

— Ask the Holy Spirit to guide you through this prayer . . .

— Think of a time in the past when your faith was very much tested, when you felt confused and at sea, perhaps desperate . . . when you needed to believe and to trust in the goodness, power and wisdom of God . . . reflect a bit on this and try to relive the experience . . .

— Take up the words of the despairing father of the very sick child: "Lord I believe, help my unbelief" . . . Say these words first with your lips, then with your heart . . . Let them come up from deep down in you . . . hear them . . . think of nothing else except what you are saying . . . just centre on the sentence . . . Let the words sink deeply into you by gently repeating the words again and again . . .

— When you feel the time is right, begin to close your prayer and thank God. . .

— Slowly and gently open your eyes and end the prayer.

Lord, you died for me on the cross

— Find a comfortable posture . . . close your eyes . . . and quieten yourself . . .

— Do one of the relaxation exercises . . .

- Take two or three deep breaths . . . then let your breathing return to its normal rhythm . . . be aware of your breathing without controlling it . . . then forget it . . .

- Ask the Holy Spirit to guide you through this prayer . . .

- Reflect for a while on the Crucifixion . . . Become aware that it was for the love of *you* . . . this was the sign, the proof, of how much he loves you . . .

- Begin to respond to this awareness by saying: "Lord you died for the love of me" . . . Keep on saying these words . . . let them seep deep into your heart . . . perhaps after a time you'd like to shorten them, expressing their essence in a few words, e.g. "for the love of me" or "you died" . . . keep on saying them . . . try not to get tired . . .

- When you feel the time is right, begin to close your prayer and thank God. . .

- Slowly and gently open your eyes and end the prayer.

You are my Shepherd – I shall not fear

- Find a comfortable posture . . . close your eyes . . . and quieten yourself . . .

- Do one of the relaxation exercises . . .

- Take two or three deep breaths . . . then let your breathing return to its normal rhythm . . . be aware of

71

your breathing without controlling it . . . then forget it
. . .

— Ask the Holy Spirit to guide you through this prayer
. . .

— Picture for yourself a shepherd with his sheep . . . see
the protection, care and love that the shepherd pro-
vides for them . . .

— Now transfer this image to Jesus the good shepherd
. . . he lays down his life for his sheep . . . he never
deserts his flock . . .

— Begin to say to Jesus: "You are my shepherd, I shall
not fear" . . . Keep on saying this sentence first clearly
and distinctly, paying attention to every word . . . then
gradually make it more automatic and reduce the
sentence to a few words but still focusing on its full
meaning: You may want to make some longer or
shorter pauses in between, and rest in the comfort that
the message gives you . . . but try not to let anything
else intrude! Just focus on "Jesus, you are my shepherd, I shall not fear" . . .

— When you feel the time is right, begin to close your
prayer and thank God. . .

— Slowly and gently open your eyes and end the prayer.

Maranatha, come Lord Jesus, come

— Find a comfortable posture . . . close your eyes . . . and
quieten yourself . . .

72

- Do one of the relaxation exercises . . .

- Take two or three deep breaths . . . then let your breathing return to its normal rhythm . . . be aware of your breathing without controlling it . . . then forget it . . .

- Ask the Holy Spirit to guide you through this prayer . . .

- You may feel empty or alone, or you may have a great longing for the Lord, then say "Maranatha, come Lord Jesus, come" . . . just slowly and gently and keep on saying the phrase . . . try not to be side-tracked, just centre on Maranatha. . . .

- When you feel the time is right, begin to close your prayer and thank God. . .

- Slowly and gently open your eyes and end the prayer.

The Master is here and is calling me

- Find a comfortable posture . . . close your eyes . . . and quieten yourself . . .

- Do one of the relaxation exercises . . .

- Take two or three deep breaths . . . then let your breathing return to its normal rhythm . . . be aware of your breathing without controlling it . . . then forget it . . .

- Ask the Holy Spirit to guide you through this prayer . . .

– Think of the scene of Martha coming to Mary her sister and telling her: "The Master is here and is calling You" . . .

– Say to yourself: "The Master is here and is calling me" . . . keep on saying these words . . . try not to get tired . . . or be distracted however difficult it feels, you may have longer or shorter pauses between the repetition if you wish . . . or you may cut the words down to one or two . . . bring them more and more into your heart and stay with them. . . .

– When you feel the time is right, begin to close your prayer and thank God. . .

– Slowly and gently open your eyes and end the prayer.

PART FIVE

Praying with the Imagination

After more than twenty years in Borneo as a missionary, I went to the United States for a spiritual renewal course. During this course we did all kinds of things that I had never done before.

One day, after doing some relaxation exercises we were asked to lie down and be still. Then we were asked in our imagination to visit a field and admire all the beautiful wild flowers and grass, and to pick one according to our liking. After looking at it from all sides, studying it and admiring it we were asked to become it, to imagine ourselves to *be* this flower, to feel how it felt. We identified with this flower for a considerable period of time. Then we returned to be ourselves and gradually ended the meditation. We then split up into groups and shared with one another what we had experienced. It was wonderful! I was amazed at what people had experienced, and how they felt when they were the flower. Most people had chosen different flowers, some a small one, some a big one, some a most beautiful one and some a very ordinary plain one.

At the start of the exercise I was feeling very annoyed and angry. I thought I had not come to do such unrealistic exercises, but to be taught and to learn. So this first exercise made little impression on me, but I decided that if others could get so much out of it, then why shouldn't I?

Fortunately, during the course of the year, we had many such journeys through the joyful and sad experiences of our lives. How much healing and wholeness resulted from these meditations nobody can tell. I certainly went away a much better integrated person with a more purposeful attitude to life and would no longer reject these meditations as meaningless.

The important point is that if such imaginative reliving of past joys and sorrows can bring so much healing and wholeness in people, how much more beneficial it could be if we tried to relive, in the same imaginative way, a biblical scene or event, or an action of Christ concerning salvation. We will need the grace of God, but if we are sincerely open to receive this grace, God will not refuse us.

HISTORICAL BACKGROUND

In his mystical treatise, *The Tree of Life*, St Bonaventure writes when dealing with the story of the three wise men: "Also you, O my soul, join the three wise men and adore together with them the humble God lying in the manger."

That phrase, "Also you, O my soul", St Bonaventure repeats over and over again in nearly every chapter. Thus we read, "Rejoice also you, O my soul, with the old Simeon and prophetess Anna, or accompany also you, O my soul, the Saviour to the river Jordan for his baptism, or Search also you, O my soul, together with the good Master the secrets of the desert".

In these sentences St Bonaventure is describing a form of prayer which today we call "Ignatian". This involves projecting ourselves into the past events of Christ's life on earth and reliving them in our imagination, so that we can draw spiritual benefit from them.

The sensible imagination is brought into play to relive the event as affectively as possible, so that real sorrow or joy, for example, are experienced as fully as possible.

This way of praying is very old, its roots going back to at least 1000 BC. Every year the Israelites would relive the marvels the Lord had done for them; these annual celebrations became a real participation in, and a reliving of, past history. For the Israelites it was not merely a remembrance. This idea was then taken over by the early monks, and further developed and practised by monks in the Middle Ages.

St Francis of Assisi in particular made much use of this way of praying. For him Christ was certainly the Lord, who even as a little child ruled from his mother's lap, as many paintings and sculptures depicted. For Francis, Christ was also the God child, whose human birth he was able to witness very vividly in his imagination. It was this child that had stretched out his hands to him, the beggar of Assisi, at Greccio to be caressed and kissed. Christ was also for Francis the king that inspired holy fear, and respect. But in addition to all this, he was also the ordinary, simple poor man who walked the streets of Palestine, whom Francis could follow and imitate. He could be present at his miracles and other wonderful deeds; could watch and grieve with him in the Garden of Olives, or accompany him to Calvary, sharing in his sufferings to such an extent that on Mount Alverna he received the stigmata.

This form of prayer spread quickly and far, and St Ignatius of Loyola, who was born in France in 1491 and died in 1556, was largely instrumental in spreading and promoting it, recommending it particularly in his booklet *The Spiritual Exercises* which became very popular.

Although in later years its popularity declined somewhat and it was superseded by a more discursive form of prayer, it never totally disappeared from the scene. We all know that Nativity and Passion plays are greatly appreciated and loved even in our own time, or that children like to act out a scene from the Bible. And many ordinary people as they read the Bible do not indulge in any profound reflections on the text, but instead relive the text as profoundly as possible with the help of their imagination.

FURTHER EXPLANATIONS

When in the gospels, sick, possessed or troubled people met Jesus and were healed and liberated from their troubles, this encounter was not a mere physical one, nor just a successful visit to a doctor. The encounter took place on a much deeper level. It was for them an encounter with Jesus that took place deep in their inner being. The gospels tell us only of the external aspects of the happening, but what really happened to these people is beyond description.

How can we then get to know the real significance of these gospel events? We will be able to penetrate their deeper meaning by thinking and reflecting on them, but only to a certain degree. The mind has its limits in these matters. But we can get beyond these limits when we no longer *just* think and reflect, but actually live ourselves into them, when we become part and parcel of the events. Then we no longer perceive them with our mind alone, but also with all our other faculties of awareness beyond our mind – the heart, the emotions, the interior senses, our power of experiencing the hidden depths of our being.

The message, or the truth, that the Evangelists convey to us is usually enfolded within a historical and tangible shell. At first we look at the shell, then we try to penetrate into the event until we begin to live it, to experience it, to identify with it, becoming part of it. In this journey inward we will begin with the more external aspect of the story and then gradually allow ourselves to sink even more deeply into its depth where the real message lies. The beauty is that in this way God can lead us to the core of his message and fill us with wisdom and understanding, without our needing to possess a special understanding of the Scriptures.

God, besides our thinking, has given us many other faculties. He has given us exterior and interior senses. He has given us a long-term memory; he has given us the faculty of imagination, with which we can visualize things, feel and notice things with our interior senses. The Latin word for picture or image is "imago" so we call the power to visualize in our mind "imagination". This power varies with people. Some have a highly developed imagination, others possess the faculty in a weaker manner, but we all possess it and can all make use of it, for it is the power that opens for us the possibility of praying imaginatively.

Now this faculty of imagination can do two things, for it is both "sensible" and "creative".

a. With the "sensible imagination" we can imagine we are really present at a scene, an event or an object. We can see, hear, talk, touch, feel, taste and smell, not with our *actual* senses but with our mysterious, interior senses. With these we can do imaginatively all and sometimes more, than we can do with our exterior senses.

b. With the "creative imagination" we can create new images by combining and rearranging old images stored in our memory. The memory supplies all the material, all the images. The imagination makes a selection, arranging and combining them according to need. That is why the new image created by the imagination can be very much like the original object or event, or it can be very much a new creation. The objective material of the imagination can be a physical object or a symbol, a story, or a past event.

So what can we do with the imagination? What are the main forms of imaginative prayer?

a. The first is "Projection". With the help of our imagination we can by-pass time and space and project ourselves back to the scene, or event, and become fully present to it, as it was, there and then.

We are present at the historical event of the past but as if it were *happening* here and now. With the help of our imagination we can relive the event in a real, effective manner. We can feel sorrow, joy, sadness, courage and can experience all the other emotions of the heart. We can see, hear, touch, feel, taste and smell for our whole being is involved. We are not onlookers at the event, but real participants. St Ignatius says in the *Spiritual Exercises* on the contemplation of the Nativity: "I will make myself a poor, little, unworthy servant, and as though present, look upon them, contemplate them, and serve them in their needs with all possible homage and reverence. I will then reflect on myself that I may reap some fruit."

b. The second is "Transposition". For instance, I can imagine Jesus walking into my room now and saying to me, "I love you – love me too". We hear his words, we hear him call us by name. We can imagine him standing at our side, or feel him laying his hands on our shoulders. But this is not just make-believe for Jesus is always walking with us through life.

c. The third is "Identification". In our imagination we can identify with the various characters in the stories and events of our prayer. We can identify with Peter as he cries out to Jesus when he is sinking, or with the poor woman caught in adultery. We can imagine that we are one of these people whom Jesus meets and helps. We experience everything that happened at that first encounter. Often, of course, we will not imagine we have the same trouble as they had, but we *feel* ourselves to be in a similar position. We can feel rejected, poor, spiritually hungry, or spiritually blind, deaf and dumb, or dead to our faith and love.

d. The fourth is "Fantasy". With our imagination we can fantasize, we can create many new situations, scenes, and images, if we give our heart the freedom to wander and explore. When we surrender ourselves to the Spirit of God, who is present not only in Scripture but also in our hearts and in the imagination of the believing pray-er, we will experience how these fantasy excursions, these wanderings of the imagination are a helpful way to deeper prayer.

e. The fifth is "Symbolic", for in our imaginative prayer we can make use of symbols and symbolic actions and allow them to play an important part in our inner life, as they do in our ordinary life. For example, in our prayer we can make use of symbols such as fire, water, food and light, or in terms of Baptism, for example, we can visualise the water of life flowing through our heart making all things new.

All that I have described above lies within the scope of our imagination, and no one must be afraid or worry that they do not have one, even if until now they have not used it in the context of prayer.

Healing of the Leper
(Mark 1:40–42)

If we want to experience the Gospel contemplatively, then it is perhaps good if we reflect at first: how can I identify with this or that person? In our, case with this leper? We can become aware that before God's holiness we all appear as "unclean". But we can also think of something else: the leper is exposed, he is excluded from the community, he is rejected. He no longer belongs to the others. He feels and experiences that he is one who no longer belongs anywhere. Perhaps we also feel in a certain way that we no longer belong. We feel excluded from many things. We feel separated from other people.

The leper was constantly aware of the fear people had when they came near him, the fear of coming in contact with him. Do we not experience the same thing? We often see the fear in the face of someone who has to meet us. He does come towards us but then he turns back. Hardly anyone comes to us without any fear. Now if we reflect on all this and let it seep into us then I think we can easily identify with the leper of the Gospel.

– Now read through the text a few times and familiarize yourself with the story, the place, the situation, the people, the occasion and all the rest. Then close the book and begin the prayer.

– Take up a comfortable posture . . . close your eyes and quieten yourself . . .

– Do one of the relaxation exercises . . .

– Become aware of the Holy Spirit living in you . . . ask him to lead and guide you through the prayer experience . . . to open you up . . .

– So now imagine you are the leper . . . sit somewhere away from the people and feel excluded from their life, interests and activities . . .

– In this situation how do you feel? . . . what do you think? . . . what is your reaction? . . . Are you angry, depressed or indifferent? . . . What do you do? . . .

– Now look up . . . you see a group of people coming towards you . . . In their midst is he of whom you have already heard – Jesus . . . You would like to come near him – can you dare to do that? . . . What will the people say? . . . So you go towards him . . . The people object . . . but what about him? . . . How does he – Jesus –

react to your coming to him? . . . What does he do? . . . He stands still and looks at you . . . See his look . . . full of love and mercy: feel and drink deeply . . . feel yourself embraced by this loving look . . . This man has compassion for me . . . other people only give me advice or help, but this men suffers with me, because he sees me suffer . . .

— In the joy that comes from him throw yourself at his feet and say to him: "Lord, if you want, you can help me, you can make me clean, you can release me from my isolation, my loneliness and depression . . . If you want you can heal me and give me peace . . .

— "If you want. I don't demand. I don't lament . . . May your will be done" . . . then wait for his decision.

— Now he comes closer to you . . . he stretches out his hand and touches your shoulder and then lays his right hand on your head . . . How do you feel? Have you ever received so much love and tenderness? . . . Bend your head a little and be quite still in order to experience for a long time this healing hand on your head . . . remain quite still and allow Jesus to heal you and strengthen you and love you . . . stay silently contemplating the healing Jesus . . .

— Now he takes his hand away from you again . . . not in order to go away but to bend down to you, to grip you with both hands and lift you up . . .

— As you stand before him and look into his face he says to you: "Come with me!" "Where to?" "To where you should be for me, at your work, at your home, at your duty" . . . Let this call of Jesus penetrate into you . . .

- Now say something like this to Jesus: "Yes Jesus, I go with you. I know that you go with me . . . I am no longer alone and rejected, but accepted into the community of people . . . You send me to them, you accompany me, you, my new friend . . . I will bring you to the people" . . .

- When you feel the time is right, begin to close your prayer and thank God. . .

- Slowly and gently open your eyes and end the meditation.

Zacchaeus
(Luke 19:1-10)

Jesus was on his way up to Jerusalem, to his being "taken up" to his death and resurrection. During this journey many things happened. As he entered Jericho the final incident took place. There was a man named Zacchaeus, a chief tax collector. The tax collectors were a despised class in Jesus's time. They enriched themselves by working for the colonial government in Rome, thus betraying their own people and nation. The prostitutes, tax collectors and public sinners were the outcasts to whom the Good News of Jesus was especially directed.

Jesus loved these people because their situation left them stripped naked of pretence and hypocrisy. They could be genuine as others often couldn't . . . The Lord had put a desire into his heart to see Jesus. He was free to respond even by making a fool of himself but this act of foolishness transformed his whole life.

The call that Jesus made to the various Apostles and to Zacchaeus he makes to us too. It is always personal and unique. Perhaps we find ourselves in a similar position to Zacchaeus? Perhaps we are also despised and rejected because of our work or sins, or perhaps we just feel rejected or excluded, apart. Jesus loves all of us. He calls us personally to be with him, to belong. Are we hearing his call? Let us join Zacchaeus and meet Jesus as he enters Jericho.

— Read through the text a few times and familiarize yourself with the story, the people, the occasion and all the rest. Then close the book and begin the prayer.

— Find a comfortable posture . . . close your eyes and quieten yourself . . .

— Do one of the relaxation exercises . . .

— Become aware of the Holy Spirit living in you . . . ask him to lead and guide you through the prayer experience . . . to open you up and free you . . .

— Now imagine Jericho . . . the houses . . . the streets . . . the traffic . . . the people . . . Compose yourself, seeing the place: What kind of place is it? . . . big – small? clean – dirty? old – new? . . . Notice the whole layout and structure of the place . . .

— Now let the whole scene become alive . . . See the people . . . How many people are there? . . . What sort of people are they? . . . Where do they come from? . . . How are they behaving? . . . What are they saying? . . .

— Where in the crowd are you? . . . What are you doing in this place? . . . Why are you there? . . . Try to view the whole scene, take an active part in it . . . Be part of the show . . . How are you feeling? . . . Do you speak to anyone? . . .

86

– Now notice Zacchaeus . . . Watch him carefully . . . What kind of man is he? . . . What does he look like? . . . What is he doing? . . . Watch the people as he pushes his way through the crowd and climbs a tree . . . What do they say? . . . What do you think of this man? . . .

– Now there is a great commotion! . . . Jesus is coming! . . . Where are you? . . . Can you see Jesus? . . . What does he look like? . . . How does he behave? . . . Does he speak, wave his hands, smile or is he serious? . . . Watch the whole scene carefully . . . Keep your eyes on Jesus . . .

– Jesus now reaches the tree where Zacchaeus is waiting . . . What does Jesus do? . . . Hear him speak . . . What does he say? . . . How does his voice sound? . . . How does Zacchaeus react? . . . How do the people react? . . . Watch them! . . . Are they happy? . . . Is Zacchaeus happy? . . .

– Now you have reached Zacchaeus' house . . . You are also invited . . . Calm yourself, look around you . . . Notice all the people and things in the house . . . Who are all the guests? . . . Where does Jesus sit? . . . Where do you sit? . . .

– What is the conversation during this time? . . . Does Jesus speak? . . . What does he say? . . . Does Zacchaeus speak? . . . Who else speaks or does something? . . .

– You are the only white person in the party. . . . Jesus comes now to you . . . How do you feel? . . . What does he say to you? . . . What do you say to him? . . . Keep on talking to him for a while . . .

- How does Jesus treat you? . . . Has he any message or advice for you? . . . What does he want of you? . . . If he has not given you a message or advice yet, ask him what he wants of you or how you can be of service to him . . .

- When you feel the time is right, begin to close your prayer and thank God. . .

- Slowly and gently open your eyes and end the meditation.

Thomas meets the Lord
(John 20:24–29)

When we pray using our imagination we must have faith. Jesus only appeared to those who had faith in him. He could only be seen by those who believed in him. He says himself: "Believe, and then you will see." You may still ask: but what proof do I have that the vision was not *produced* by my faith? This is irrelevant. We are not interested in attaining proof. If we believe we will know. If we love a person we know his beauty.

Thomas did not see the risen Lord until he had faith. Jesus said to him "Blessed are those who have not seen yet believe". Because when we believe, we will see. Perhaps we find ourselves in the same situation as Thomas? Perhaps we do not see! Perhaps we do not meet the Lord in Prayer? Perhaps we have no faith or we are afraid to imagine. In whatever way we may resemble Thomas let us go with him now to the Upper Room and with him meet the Lord in prayer. Perhaps we shall then also be able to say; "My Lord and my God". But if you still have doubts or feel discouraged don't worry, but keep on praying. Doubts need not discourage us but can help us grow and mature in faith.

– Read through the text a few times and familiarize yourself with the story, the place, the situation, the people. Then close the book and begin the prayer.

– Take up a comfortable posture . . . close your eyes and quieten yourself . . .

– Do one of the relaxation exercises . . .

– Become aware of the Holy Spirit living in you . . . ask him to lead and guide you through the prayer experience . . . to open you up and make you free. . .

– Now project yourself back to the upper room where the Apostles are gathered. See them in that room and imagine yourself to be there . . .

– Look around in the room . . . what do you see? . . . See everything . . . the table, the walls, the lamps . . . Become aware of the closed door . . . Do you feel more secure with closed doors? . . . What are you afraid of? . . .

– Now see the Apostles talking to one another . . . What are they saying? . . . Who are you among these Apostles? . . . Perhaps the one who does not yet fully believe in the Risen Lord? . . . Think of your scepticism, your halfheartendess, perhaps your doubts . . . Are you not Thomas? . . .

– Has the door opened yet? . . . No. It is still locked . . . But Jesus has come in. He stands in the middle of the

89

room. Everybody is shocked and terrified . . . Look at him! See him as you have never seen him before . . . See the light in his face . . . See the glimmer in his eyes . . .

– Listen and hear him say, "Peace, peace be with you . . ."

– Let go of all fear and terror, all that initially overwhelmed you when he first appeared. Let this wonderful word "peace" penetrate you . . . Let yourself be totally filled with it . . .

– Become aware of your heart . . . Feel how little peace there is in it . . . how you are still troubled and harassed by what lies within you, and how anxious and fearful you are of the future . . . Feel how dissatisfied you still are because so many expectations that you constantly look for in your neighbours, or perhaps your friends . . . or even your family . . . are not fulfilled, and so many earthly wishes are still unanswered.

– But now let go of everything that is unimportant or is bothering you because you see Jesus in front of you, saying: "Peace be with you . . ."

– Peace! . . . As you inhale, let this peace enter and penetrate deep into you . . . When you exhale, just rest in this peace . . .

– Let a great and peaceful rest fill you, so that everything around you loses its importance, fades away . . . just feel yourself in a room of peace . . . A room that is empty yet full of light . . . For he who says: "I am the light of the World" forms this room around you . . . let your heart bathe in it and become ever more peaceful.

— Slowly wake up again . . . see the Apostles, the room and Jesus in his physical form before you . . .

— Now Jesus moves, he stretches out his hands and shows you his wounds . . . He comes still closer to you . . . What does this gesture mean? . . . Is it to blame you? . . . No. He just wants to meet you in your helplessness. For now you no longer doubt, but you believe . . . Still more, you love and would like to touch him in love . . . But can you do that? . . . His coming closer to you says: "Yes you may" . . .

— Stretch out your hands and put your fingers in his wounds . . . not to prove the truth, but in order to feel and touch him, who loves you so much . . .

— Now say, . . . Lord, I not only like to touch you, I would even like to embrace you with the arms of my heart . . . to press you to my heart, to take you in and keep you there you whom I call: My Lord and My God!" Stay with him and adore him! . . .

— When you feel the time is right, begin to close your prayer and thank God. . .

— Slowly and gently open your eyes and end the meditation.

In Search of God

It is important when we pray imaginatively that we really *do* imagine or fantasize. Try not to remember things or places, try to imagine them, and try not to be conscious of your present surroundings . . . actually be in your fantasy place. So if we imagine we are on the sea-shore we imagine hearing the roar of the waves, and feel the sun beating on our bodies, we feel the touch of the hot sand under our feet . . . and as a result we experience all the feelings that we have previously experienced . . .

Let us now go in search of God. We do not know where he waits for us. We might find him in a place where we do not expect to find him, which may be very revealing.

– Find a comfortable posture . . . close your eyes . . . and quieten yourself . . .

– Do one of the relaxation exercises . . .

– Become aware of the Holy Spirit living in you . . . ask him to guide you through the prayer experience. Ask him to open you up and free you. . .

– Imagine yourself sitting on top of a mountain . . . the sun is just going down . . . it is a most beautiful spectacle . . . watch it and enjoy it . . . forget all your worries and problems and let yourself be filled with this wonderful moment . . .

– As you awake from this deep contemplation of wonder, peace and well-being, you hear footsteps . . . as you look up you see in the semi-dusk an old man coming to you . . . You recognize him as a holy man, a hermit who lives in the region . . . He comes up to you and says gently and warmly: "If you go down to the city you will find God." Then he walks away . . .

– How do you feel? . . . What is going through your mind? . . . Do you want to go down or would you rather stay on the mountain? . . .

– Whatever way you feel . . . I want you to go down in search of God . . . What are your feelings? . . . Is your journey down easy or difficult? . . .

– You have now come to the outskirts of the city . . . You have to decide where to go in search of God . . . Do not go where you want to go . . . Take your time and listen . . . let the Holy Spirit lead you . . . go where the heart tells you . . . do not moralize over where you ought to go . . . Just go where your heart tells you . . .

– Where has your heart led you? . . . What is happening there? . . . What do you find? . . . What do you do there? . . . Do you find God? . . . In what way? . . . In a person . . . in a situation . . . in a symbol? . . . Take your time and be receptive. God can be found in many ways . . . keep your eyes and ears open . . .

– Have you found God? . . . If you have, stay with him, listen to him, or watch him, speak with him . . . Put yourself into his shoes, identify with him . . . If you have not yet found him go on searching, follow the lead of your heart . . . Do not be anxious, you will find him somewhere . . .

– Take leave from him . . . say something to him and give your emotions a free hand . . . do not be ashamed to express your feelings . . . . . .

– When you feel the time is right, begin to close your prayer and thank God. . .

– Slowly and gently open your eyes and end the meditation.

The living flame of love

The title of this meditation is from St John of the Cross, but the inspiration is from the *Cloud of Unknowing*. The cloud speaks of a **blind stirring** of love in the centre of our being. We will try to contemplate this living flame of love which can stir our heart. . . .

— Find a comfortable posture . . . close your eyes . . . and quieten yourself . . .

— Do one of the relaxation exercises . . .

— Become aware of the Holy Spirit living in you . . . ask him to guide you through the prayer experience . . . Ask him to open you up and make you free. . .

— Now start a long journey . . . go down into the depths of your being . . . It is very dark . . . but you grope along and at the end, at the very centre of your being, you find a living flame of love shooting upwards to God . . .

— Watch the flame . . . get the feel of its rhythm and tune into it . . .

— Now put a word or a short phrase to the rhythm of the flame . . . such as: Jesus – Abba – Come Holy Spirit – My God and My All –

— Listen closely to this word or phrase as it is being uttered in the depth of your being . . . Do not say it out loud, but hear it faintly coming from far away, from your depths . . .

— Hear it become louder and louder . . . filling your whole being . . . your head, your chest, your stomach, the whole of your body, the whole room . . . It grows

94

more and more intense and fills the whole earth and the heavens, so that eventually the whole universe resounds with this word or phrase that comes from the depth of your being . . .

— Feel its sound all over the earth . . . perhaps say it yourself lovingly . . . identify with it and rest in it . . .

— When you feel the time is right, begin to close your prayer and thank God. . .

— Slowly and gently open your eyes and end the meditation.

My heart is a beautiful garden

— Find a comfortable posture . . . close your eyes . . . and quieten yourself . . .

— Do one of the relaxation exercises . . .

— Become aware of the Holy Spirit living in you . . . ask him to guide you through the prayer experience, ask him to open you up and free you. . .

— Imagine a beautiful garden . . . walk in it . . . see all its beauty and enjoy it . . . immerse yourself in the beauty of this garden . . . lose yourself in it . . .

— Imagine that this garden is your heart and Christ walks around in it, enjoying all the flowers and beauty . . . go around with him, keep him company and take part and share in his joy . . . Do not be afraid to show him all of it, even the least of its contents . . . or just rest in the joy that the Lord finds in your garden . . .

– Now say goodbye to your Lord who has revealed himself to you and with whom you have spent all this time . . .

– When you feel the time is right, begin to close your prayer and thank God. . .

– Slowly and gently open your eyes and end the prayer.

Forgiveness and healing

Really to forgive is a very difficult thing to do. Certainly with our own strength and power it is practically impossible. There may be many of us who have never really forgiven. We try to forget, we brush the offence aside and say, "forget about it", or "it is all right" etc. but we have not really forgiven and so there is still anger, hurt and resentment in us. These are like festering sores in us, making us feel ill at times. They block and hinder us from making progress in our prayer-life and make us feel despondent.

I am quite sure many people would pay a high price to get rid of this non-forgiveness and be able to forgive and forget. Not everyone can go to professional counsellors and psychiatrists etc., to seek help, not all find sufficient help in confession, and so they carry the burden for years in their heart. They are angry even with the dead.

I know by experience that it is very difficult to forgive all by ourselves, but I also know that by the help of God all things are possible. I have seen great miracles happening in this respect. People have given up great hatred and resentment with the help of Jesus. One cannot look into the eyes of Jesus and still hate. I am suggesting here a form of prayer that has helped many people: . . .

— Find a comfortable posture . . . close your eyes . . . and quieten yourself . . .

— Do one of the relaxation exercises . . .

— Ask the Holy Spirit to guide you in this prayer . . . put yourself into the hands of the Spirit and trust him . . .

— Now go up to Calvary and place yourself before the Cross . . . Look up to the Cross and into the face of Jesus . . . just look at his face . . . what do you see? . . . Let yourself be touched and moved by his great love for you and keep on looking . . .

— As you look at him notice your "enemy" also coming there, standing somewhere beside you, also looking up to the Cross . . . Notice Jesus turning a bit and looking upon your "enemy" . . . Watch his face . . . his expression . . . his love and goodness . . .

— Now let all the anger, resentment, hatred and all negativeness you feel for your "enemy" come up and out . . . tell Jesus what you think of him or her . . . what he or she has done to you . . . how he or she has hurt you . . . damaged you and how much you suffer because of him or her . . . tell Jesus that you do not understand that he can love that person who has done so much harm to you . . . Just let it all come out . . . give vent to your anger . . . give vent to your tears and any other emotion . . . take your time.

— When you have finished look again at Jesus . . . listen to him . . . what does his expression tell you? . . . Keep on looking at him . . . his look will eventually soften your anger and you may be able to have some form of reconciliation.

– Perhaps you are able to tell your "enemy" that you forgive him, to look into his face . . . to shake hands with him or perhaps you are able to embrace him and cry and really forgive him or her . . . Do just what you can do . . .

– Then praise and thank the Lord . . . ask him for further help . . .

– Slowly and gently open your eyes and end the prayer.

N.B. You may have to do the exercise more than once. Perhaps you are not able to forgive totally the first time. Do only what you can, but do not give up until you have forgiven totally. You will be grateful afterwards. Do not think because the method is simple it is not effective. It is, but, like all therapy, it is also hard and painful. Dying to self is always painful . . . Have courage and persevere . . .

Praying for Ourselves

We all have needs, desires and longings. We are short of so many things, we need to pray for forgiveness, for mercy. We often lack faith, hope and charity. We may be sick or in great difficulty of one kind or another. The fact is that we depend on God for everything. He is our Father, we are his children. Jesus tells us to pray, to ask, to seek and to knock. The Father will never refuse us what we ask in Jesus's name. He just wants us to come to him with great trust and confidence. To trust him is the greatest thing we can do.

But the problem still remains – how to pray, how to ask. Some people keep on with a request, pleading, nagging and pestering God for what they want. Jesus tells us that we should not use many words, but go into our heart and be there with the Lord, for he knows all that we need. This way of praying for things is more contemplative, without many words or with none at all. Try it out and don't worry if you have not told God everything. Some people worry that they have not made it clear enough to God. He knows all, just love him and trust him. . . .

– Find a comfortable posture . . . close your eyes . . . and quieten yourself . . .

– Do one of the relaxation exercises . . .

– Ask the Holy Spirit to pray in you too and let yourself be guided by him . . .

– Put your hands on your lap and hold them in the form of a cup . . . now fill this cup with all your requests, desires and longings . . . Put all you want to pray for into the cup of your hands . . .

– Become fully aware of all that is in the cup . . . own it and identify with it, make it entirely yours . . . Don't break your heart over it but just be aware of all, and that you own all . . .

– Now come into the presence of God . . . love him and allow him to love you, praise him, just remain in silent contemplation with him . . . be with him as he wants you to be with him . . . don't think of the things in the cup . . . only think of the Lord . . . concentrate on him alone . . . Stay like that as long as you can . . . . . .

– When you feel the time is right, begin to close your prayer and thank God. . .

– Slowly and gently open your eyes and end the prayer.

Prayers of Intercession

Teilhard de Chardin, who died in 1955, says in one of his books that while a nun was praying in a desert chapel, all the forces of the universe seemed to re-organise themselves according to the desire of that little nun praying, and the axis of the world seemed to pass through that chapel. He says: "Nothing is so powerful on earth as purity and prayer."

Prayer for others, or prayer of intercession, has always played an important role in many people's lives. Moses stood before God to intercede for his people; St Paul was a great man of prayer. We don't know what Jesus did on the mountain tops and the desert places, nor what he did during his long hours of prayer, but we can presume that he spent many hours in praying for the people he came to be with and to save.

Some people are led into deep contemplative prayer, into deep union with God, in order to pray for others. It often leads into a deeper union with God, for the more we lavish God's blessing on others, the more he will flood our own hearts and life with his blessing. Once we have experienced the power there is in prayer and the wonders God does through our prayer, we will not easily give it up though we may be tempted to from time to time. . . .

— Find a comfortable posture . . . close your eyes . . . and quieten yourself . . .

— Do one of the relaxation exercises . . .

— Ask the Holy Spirit to pray in you, . . . Let him guide you . . .

— Think of the people, the communities, the countries or nations you want to pray for . . . allow them all to come vividly before you . . . see their needs and their problems . . . live yourself into their needs . . . or, as I do, try to become them, unite yourself with them, identify yourself with them . . .

— Turn to God . . . ask him to fill you with his power, his energy, his life, and grace . . . feel yourself being flooded with it . . . feel yourself becoming more and more part of him, taken over by God . . .

— Imagine the people you want to pray for gathered before you, stretch out your hands over them and let the energy and grace of God flow out through you to them . . . keep your gaze, constantly on God, not on those you are praying for . . . Stay with him all the time, and do not worry about the people. . . .

— When you feel the time is right, begin to close your prayer and thank God. . .

— Slowly and gently open your eyes and end the prayer.

PART SIX

Praying with the Sense of Hearing

When Pope John Paul II visited Germany the following incident took place.

A bus load of people was on its way to see the Pope, but inside the bus the atmosphere was far from pleasant. The driver was not in the least interested in seeing the Pope. He was grumbling and even cursing all the time, objecting to the personality cult, the wastage of money and all sorts of other things. He totally disagreed with the Pope's visit, which created a very unpleasant atmosphere. On arrival at the airport the people left the bus so that they could obtain a view of the Pope when he left the plane. The driver remained in the bus. After some time the helicopter carrying the Pope arrived and landed quite near to the bus. On emerging from the helicopter the Pope looked around and spotted the driver in his bus. He then approached and having greeted him in a most friendly manner enquired after his wife and children, and as he left gave him his blessing.

When the people returned to the bus they found the driver in tears. He said: "The Pope spoke to me. He did not ask me whether or not I was a Catholic, neither did he ask why I did not accompany you. He spoke to me as a friend and blessed me."

One wonders how often this driver will tell that story as the years go by and how often he will recall this memory in order to re-experience the joy of that momentous event in his life.

When we speak of "Heart Hearing" we do not mean hearing the Word of God, as when scripture is read aloud or we listen to a sermon. Nor do we mean hearing an inner voice. What we mean is that we imagine we hear God or Jesus addressing us personally with a word or sentence.

So the first experience in this process will be the realization that God *is addressing me personally*.

It can be like a new injection of life when we imagine that God or Jesus is speaking to us in a single word.

To put this into practice involves the following. We need to take up a comfortable position, become very quiet and relaxed. We remain still, enjoy the moment of the first surprise that God is speaking to us. This can be a moment of deep happiness and we try to keep the image constantly before us, saying over and over again, in quiet rhythm – "He is speaking to me! He is speaking to me!"

The next step will be to listen to the words he is saying to me. Such words are found in abundance in the Old and New Testaments.

We can also hear Jesus speak to us in silence. Let us take some ordinary, everyday experiences. Sometimes we may experience an oppressive silence from the person to whom we are speaking, or we may feel that a person whom we have hurt answers with a cold or reproachful silence. At times we may ask someone for something and not even get an answer. Perhaps we have asked him for something to which we have no right, or for something that he wants to keep as a personal secret, or we can be met with a waiting silence, as if some initiative is expected from us.

We have all as children had the experience that when we did something wrong our mothers did not at once apportion blame or punishment, but just gave a sad look in silence. Yet we felt that it was not a reproachful silence, it was a forgiving one. As we grow up with love for our parents, or for others, we notice that there are times when we could just sit together silently, not because we had nothing to say but simply because there was no need for words. We were together in a loving silence.

We can experience these different kinds of silence with Jesus. We will never find him coldly silent but there could well be a reproachful silence. Often we find in prayer that when we ask Jesus for something, he keeps silent. He does not answer, perhaps because we would not understand, or perhaps because we are not yet ready for it. Again, it could be that he deliberately wants to leave us in the dark for our personal growth, or it may well be that he wants to show himself at this time as the unapproachable, the unknowable, the all-transcendent.

On other occasions he lets us wait because he wants us to take the first step. Most often we will find that he keeps silent in forgiveness, or we may also experience deep feelings of security, protection and of being lovingly embraced in his silence.

To conclude with a word of caution. Some people have such a highly developed imagination that they think they not only hear music in prayer, but also what they take to be lengthy revelations from God, Jesus or Mary. I am not talking of such phenomena here. Our "heart hearing" is first of all nourished by and thrives in our natural power to remember words and stories from the Bible.

Though it might be wonderful to hear heavenly music in prayer, the essentials are and always will be, to be spoken to by God in the true sense of the word and hear and listen to the words of Jesus in peace and quietness.

"Be not afraid, it is I"
(John 6:15–21; Matthew 14:22–32; Mark 6:45–52)

When Jesus walked over the water and came towards their boat, the Disciples were frightened because they thought it was a ghost. But Jesus called out to them and said: "Do not be afraid, it is I."

Maybe the ghost that we sometimes see in our life consists in the fact that we no longer understand what is happening to us, that we are so entangled and caught up with ourselves that we don't know a way out any more. How can what has happened to us be from God? In such situations we have a thousand questions to put to him, but he does not answer. Instead he comes personally before us and says "Be not afraid, it is I".

Try not to ignore this by asking more questions, but try to accept the answer which for the moment may say little to your mind. Imagine him standing before you and saying, "Do not be afraid, it is I". Your mind may still understand little, but your heart may slowly accept the answer and say "yes" to the one who stands before you. With this "yes" all your fears will be gone, but it will take time. . . .

– Find a comfortable posture . . . close your eyes . . . and quieten yourself . . .

– Do one of the relaxation exercises . . .

– Become aware of the Holy Spirit living in you . . . ask him to guide you through this prayer. . .

– Imagine the situation in which the Apostles found themselves . . . Where were they? . . . What frightened them? . . . Who was the ghost they saw? . . .

– Think of your own situation . . . Why are you afraid? . . . What is the ghost in your life? . . .

– Imagine Jesus approaching you and calling out to you . . . "Do not be afraid, it is I" . . . Allow these words to penetrate your heart . . . do not reject them as nonsense . . . listen to them for a long time . . . Even if you do not understand them let your heart accept them . . . Listen to these words as long as you can . . . let them seep into your heart . . .

– When you feel the time is right, begin to close your prayer and thank God. . .

– Slowly and gently open your eyes and end the prayer.

"Peace be with you"
(John 20:19–25; Luke 24:36–43)

John and Luke tell us that after the Resurrection Jesus appeared to the Apostles and greeted them with the words "Peace be with you!" These words he wants to say to us also, especially when we find ourselves in a similar situation to the Apostles: fearful, down-hearted, hopeless and withdrawn, or afraid of people . . . We too can imagine how Jesus suddenly stands before us and says to us: "Peace be with you!" We can try to keep before our eyes this awareness of Jesus standing before us for a long time, by constantly thinking of it, and over and over again repeating the words "Peace be with you!" The longer we do this the better it is for the words will penetrate ever more deeply into our hearts, and it is there that they will convince us that it is true that Jesus is peace, and that he gives us his peace if we are only convinced of it. . . .

— Find a comfortable posture . . . close your eyes . . . and quieten yourself . . .

— Do one of the relaxation exercises . . .

— Now become aware of the Holy Spirit living in you . . . ask him to guide you through this prayer . . .

— Place yourself in the Upper Room where the Apostles are gathered . . . imagine the place . . . the situation . . . the terrified Apostles . . . in the middle of all this Jesus appears and says: "Peace be with you!" . . .

— Now see your own situation . . . what makes you afraid? . . . Is it the people and the world around you? . . . Is it your social problems . . . the future . . . a sickness . . . sin . . . or what else? . . .

— Into this situation imagine that Jesus comes and stands before you and says to you: "Peace be with you!" . . .

— Keep on saying these words in your heart . . . Keep on hearing the words again and again . . . let them well up from deep within you . . . do not argue . . . try not to doubt them . . . just gently and quietly repeat the words and listen to them . . . again and again . . . . . .

– When you feel the time is right, begin to close your prayer and thank God. . .

– Slowly and gently open your eyes and end the prayer.

"I am the way"
(John 14:6)

In the gospels we find several sayings that Jesus applies to himself. They all begin with "I". In these sayings Jesus calls himself the Bread of Life – The Light of the World – The Door – The Good Shepherd – The Resurrection and The Life – The Way, The Truth and The Life.

We could make a study of these phrases . . . But we don't want to do this here. In heart-hearing we do not so much think about the words as listen to them. We are not out to discover the meaning of "way" or "truth" or "life", but we want to **experience Jesus** as he says these things of himself.

We must therefore imagine Jesus very close to us, we must look at him with our heart, with our inner faculty of seeing and then, again and again, hear one of these "I" sentences coming from his mouth. As we hear one of them over and over again in our heart we will surely understand something of its meaning, but even more will we be impressed and touched by the person of Jesus himself.

Let us try it out with the word "Way". . . .

– Find a comfortable posture . . . close your eyes . . . and quieten yourself . . .

– Do one of the relaxation exercises . . .

– Become aware of the Holy Spirit living in you . . . ask him to guide you through this prayer . . . you cannot pray without his help . . .

– Imagine as vividly as possible Jesus standing before you . . . you don't need to see a figure or an image . . . just be very much *aware* that he is standing before you . . .

– Now hear him say "I am the Way" with your inner ear . . . with your heart . . .

– Say these words gently to yourself until they penetrate deep into your heart and you hear their echo coming from within you. Keep on listening to these words . . . allow your heart to accept them and believe them and you may gradually experience how much Jesus attracts you as the way . . .

– When you feel the time is right, begin to close your prayer and thank God. . .

– Slowly and gently open your eyes and end the prayer.

God sings all songs and plays all music

It is not always necessary to hear words in order to become aware of God's presence. Music and sounds can also help us to experience it, for in the world of sounds and music there are many opportunities to pray, to hear God, the singer and musician.

People often complain about the sounds around them, the traffic in the streets, the blare of a radio, a door banging, or a telephone bell ringing. These noises seem to distract them, but this need not be the case. If we learn to take all these sounds into prayer, we will discover that there is a deep silence in the heart of them all.

We must also keep in mind that God is the singer of all songs and the player of all music. God not only lets the rain fall and the sun shine, he also produces all the sounds around us so that we may hear them first with our ears and then with our hearts, as we hear God speak to us in them. It might be helpful to have some music for this prayer exercise as not all the sounds I mention will be readily available! . . .

— Find a comfortable posture . . . close your eyes . . . and quieten yourself . . .

— Do one of the relaxation exercises . . .

— Become aware of the Holy Spirit living in you . . . ask him to guide you through this prayer experience, ask him to help you hear the whispering of God in the sounds . .

— Now listen to all the sounds around you . . . the big and small, the near and the distant . . . try to hear the different qualities of the sounds, the pitch and intensity . . . try to keep up with all the sounds you can hear . . .

— Now pick one sound you like: perhaps the sound of water or the wind, some music, or singing. (At this point you may need to turn your music on.)

— Then listen to the beauty of the noise and be filled and touched by it.

– In all these sounds God is present . . . if you listen long enough you will hear his voice and recognize the singer . . . So, rest in listening to one or other sound as long as you can . . . do not strain or be tense . . . just relax and listen, and one day God will show himself in the sound of what you are hearing . . .

– When you feel the time is right, begin to close your prayer and thank God. . .

– Slowly and gently open your eyes and end the prayer.

Listen to the silence of God

As there is often silence between us human beings, so can there be silence between God and us.

Now, all these silences we can also experience in our prayer. We often ask God something and he does not seem to answer for various reasons; he wants us to wait; he wants to keep us in the dark as not all knowledge is good for us. At times his silence expresses mercy and forgiveness, at other times it may be reproachful and is meant to lead us to repentance; or sometimes it may just be a wonderful and loving silence in which we feel as if we were in heaven. All silences of God tell us something, though we may sometimes think the meaning hard to find.

Let us meditate on this silence. . . .

– Find a comfortable posture . . . close your eyes . . . and quieten yourself . . .

– Do one of the relaxation exercises . . .

– Become aware of the Holy Spirit living in you . . . ask him to guide you in your prayer experience so that you may hear God speaking to you in the silence . . .

– Imagine Jesus standing before you . . . but he says nothing . . . look at him . . . see his expression . . . just stay with this silence . . . let it speak to you . . . after a time you may realize what the Lord wants to tell you . . . Let Him do to you what He wants with His silence . . . These silent moments are very precious . . . so do not dread them . . . Stay with the silence as long as you can . . .

– When you feel the time is right, begin to close your prayer and thank God. . .

– Slowly and gently open your eyes and end the prayer.

"Your sins are forgiven"
(Luke 7:36–50)

Julian of Norwich tells us that "Sin is the greatest scourge with which any chosen soul can be struck. This scourge can chastise us terribly and damage us in our own sight to such an extent that sometimes we may think we are not worth anything except to sink into hell. But then repentance comes to us by the touch of the Holy Spirit who changes the bitterness into hope for God's mercy. Our wounds begin to heal and our soul, turned to the life of Holy Church, begins to revive.

"By the Holy Spirit we are led to confession, willingly to confess our sins, and to do this openly and truthfully, with great sorrow and great shame, because we have so befouled the fair image of God. Then we are ready to take on any penance the confessor imposes on us for our sins.

"When it seems to us that we are nearly forsaken and cast away because of our sins and that we discover it so, our Good Lord holds us tenderly and protects us. Then because of being humbled by all these troubles we are raised high in God's sight by his grace."

By contrition we are made pure
By compassion we are made ready
and by true longing for God we are made worthy.

— We must firmly believe that God is never angry with us or rejects us. He always loves us as his beloved children. Nothing can separate us from his love and he always forgives us our sins, for he is full of mercy and compassion.

— Read slowly through the Bible passage referred to above . . .

— Find a comfortable posture . . . close your eyes . . . and quieten yourself . . .

— Do one of the relaxation exercises . . .

— Become aware of the Holy Spirit living in you . . . ask him to guide you, to help you hear Jesus saying to you: "Your Sins Are Forgiven" . . .

— Put yourself for a moment into the situation of Mary Magdalene . . . her sinfulness . . . her woundedness and brokenness, her pain and suffering because of her sins . . . become aware of the task which she must have felt she had to do, and how loathsome she appeared to herself to be . . .

113

— Become aware of your own situation . . . your sinful state, the guilt you feel and the pain and suffering you endure . . .

— Now, look up and see Jesus standing before you . . . He looks at you with pity and compassion, not blame or anger, and full of love he says to you: "Your Sins Are Forgiven" . . . Hear this well . . . repeat it over and over in your mind . . . let it penetrate deep into your being . . . stay with it, listening to it as long as you can . . . you will gradually come to believe and accept that the words are *really* true, he has *really* forgiven you and healed you, and he loves you . . .

— Begin to say goodbye . . . what did Mary Magdalene do? . . . You do what you feel and think is right for you to do . . .

— Slowly and gently open your eyes and end the prayer.

PART SEVEN

Praying with the Sense of Touch

A hospital chaplain once wrote: "When I am making my rounds it often happens that I find myself at my wit's end trying to find something suitable to say to the patients by way of help or consolation. Often the patients are no longer able to understand what I am trying to say, and although I want to communicate, I sometimes feel that my words are inappropriate. There is, however, something I can do to communicate. I can lay my hand on the patient's forehead and take his hand and in this way let him feel that he is not alone in his suffering, and that someone is with him and feels for him."

This shows us that we can make contact with people not only by means of words and looks, but also with the sense of touch. But does this hold good only for the physical world or does it apply to the spiritual area as well?

Jesus came into the world to bring the good news of salvation. How did he do so? In the first instance, by preaching. But there was something more – he laid his hands on people – he touched them. He grasped their hands, lifted them up or led them aside. He took children in his arms and embraced them. We read how he touched the sick, laid his hands on the eyes of the blind, the ears of the deaf and the tongues of the dumb. After the Transfiguration the three Disciples fell to the ground in fear

115

and awe. Jesus came to them, touched them and said: "Rise and have no fear."

There are many stories in the gospels which describes Jesus touching people or laying his hands on them. He took Peter's mother-in-law by the hand, lifted her up and cured her of her fever. There is the striking scene of Peter jumping into the lake and walking on the water. When he became afraid and began to sink, Jesus at once stretched out his hand and held him. There is the moving story of the twelve-year old daughter of Jairus, who was already dead by the time that Jesus arrived on the scene. He went to her head, took her by the hand and restored her to life.

What can we in the twentieth century learn from all this? We too, by using our imagination, can see, hear, touch and feel Jesus. When we pray, we can become aware of Jesus's hands being laid on us, we can experience his touch, his supporting grasp, and even his embrace. It might help here to spend some time reflecting on the hands of Jesus.

Jesus worked with his hands for many years as a carpenter. During his public life those hands became very much hands of healing and blessing. He constantly raised them to heaven in prayer and laid them on the sick to heal and console them. With them he blessed the loaves and the fishes and handed them out to the crowds. At the Last Supper those same hands took the bread, blessed and broke it in order to offer, through it, himself for us all. With those hands he touched and blessed so many people and things. They were pierced for us with nails and then shown to the Apostles as a sign of his resurrection.

JESUS TOUCHES US

Let us now try to imagine Jesus *touching* us with his holy hands, which will make us aware of his presence, of his nearness to us. This is something that it is often difficult to feel in the business and concerns of our daily life.

Thus we remain still and very quiet to savour how vividly Jesus touches us. We feel his hands on us and concentrate our complete attention on his touch. If we get distracted we once more centre our whole attention on the experience of his hands touching us. We may also try to express in a few words what we are experiencing or would like to experience: "I feel your touch, O Lord".

For some considerable time we should relish this experience, and then gradually allow to surface all that Jesus's touch arouses within us – awe, joy, reverence, happiness, perhaps just a feeling of well-being. Or it may be that he releases some past sorrow or sadness, some hurt or anxieties, but we need not worry, for whatever is exposed he can comfort and heal.

The ministry of laying on of hands has become very popular recently. I know of several doctors who lay hands on their patients and pray over them, not primarily as a cure but for strength to bear the sickness. Many groups of people do this too. The Charismatic Renewal Movement uses intercessory prayer a great deal, along with the laying on of hands. From the time of the apostles the laying on of hands has been an integral part of the ordination ceremony for the priesthood. We are all familiar with a mother's way of laying her hands on her child, of holding him, when he is sick or hurt or upset.

When I pray for people, I try to identify myself with them as much as I can. I then ask Jesus to lay his hands on me and allow his power, energy and life to flow into me and fill me, making me alive through and through, burning away all that is sick or sinful, making me whole.

When we take or hold another person's hand we can mean many things. We may be saying: "Come with me", or "Come and I will give you relief from what troubles you". We can also mean: "I am standing beside you", or "I am holding on to you to give you support to prevent you from falling." When we visit a sick person we may want to say: "I am with you. I should like to console you, I should like to give you hope." When we say goodbye to somebody by taking their hand we want to say: "Whatever you do or wherever you go, may all go well for you."

We see then how much meaning there can be in a simple handshake, and how much more meaning and power there can be when we feel Jesus taking our hands.

Jesus did not talk continually about love and friendship, but he gave ample demonstrations of his love, as we can see in his healings, in the way he dealt with sinners and when he took children into his arms and embraced them. And there is no reason why *we* cannot imagine ourselves to be the children whom Jesus took into his arms. Perhaps we find it hard to see ourselves as children because we are already adults, but within us all there is the child who can respond to Jesus's personal touch and love.

The sense of touch

Perhaps it would be good if we start with becoming more aware of the sense of touch in general. Our sense of

touch is so often deadened by not paying enough attention to it, by living too much in the mind. We miss out on a
lot of things because of this certainly in our prayer life we
are handicapped because of it.

In this first exercise it is important that we learn to feel
the touch of things. There are people who are hardly
able to feel their limbs. They know with their mind where
they are, they have a mental picture of them, but they do
not *feel* them. We must not only think and talk, but we
must also feel, sense, love and become aware for it is here
that contemplation is born. A good way to become more
aware of our sense of touch is to become sensitive to all
the various sensations in our body, and so I hope this first
exercise will help. . . .

— Find a comfortable posture . . . close your eyes . . . and
quieten yourself . . .

— Do one of the relaxation exercises . . .

— Become aware of the Holy Spirit living in you . . . ask
him to help you to become aware of the various sensations in your body . . .

— Now become aware of the touch of your clothes on
your shoulders . . . or your back touching the back of
the chair . . . feel the hands touching each other . . .
become aware of your thighs pressing against your
chair . . . feel the feet touching your shoes or the
ground . . . become aware of your sitting position . . .
just become aware of all these sensations of touch . . .
do this slowly several times . . .

— Feel the breeze as it caresses your body . . . feel the
heat of the sun or the fireplace . . . feel the cold or

warm air around you . . . feel the texture and tempera-
ture of the object you are touching . . . feel all the
things you are wearing or come in contact with . . .

— Become aware of all the different touches and sensations you can feel . . . just move around your body
from one sensation to another as you feel them . . . but
just notice them quietly . . .

— If you do this over and over again, and within your
daily life as well, you will notice how much more alive
you become, how much more in the present you begin
to live . . .

— Slowly and gently open your eyes and end the exercise.

Sensing God's touch in creation

People are longing for God. They want to meet him.
They want to experience him, to come into contact with
him. We are inclined to think that this is very difficult and
complicated, or only for holy people. But contact with
God is a grace, a gift from God, and is available to
everyone. Nothing can bring about this contact – only he
can bring that about. But we can open ourselves to it, we
can facilitate the work of God. Really it is very simple. We
need to do so little. We only need to quieten ourselves,
become still and aware of something as simple as the feel
of our hand. For in this simple illustration of awareness
we have God, living and working in us, touching us,
intensely near us. For God is in all things and all things
are in God.

- Find a comfortable posture . . . close your eyes . . . and quieten yourself . . .

- Do one of the relaxation exercises . . .

- Become aware of the Holy Spirit living in you . . . ask him to make you aware of the various sensations in your body, of God being in all things, creating them, dwelling in them and working in them . . .

- Become aware of as many sensations as you can in your body . . . do this for some time . . .

- Think and become aware that every sensation you feel, no matter how light or subtle, is the result of a biochemical reaction that could not exist without God's almighty power . . . So now feel God at work in all the various sensations . . . in every single one of them . . .

- Feel him touching you with each single sensation he produces: rough, smooth, pleasurable, painful . . .

- Now feel yourself being energized, empowered, enlivened by the touch of his power . . . feel the energy, the divine life going into you and penetrating all the parts of your body as he touches you . . .

- In your mind you may also reach out and touch somebody, feeling the power flowing out from you into that person . . .

- Say goodbye to the God whom you have met in this prayer experience . . . express to him what you want to say to him, praising and thanking him . . .

- Slowly and gently open your eyes and end the prayer.

The hands of Jesus

The people at the time of Jesus were not only able to see and hear Jesus, but they were able to touch him, to feel his hands on them, even to feel his embrace.

If the people then could do all these things then we must be able to do them as well in some way. In our prayers we are able to see and hear Jesus with our inner eyes and ears, with the heart. We are also able to touch and feel him with our inner faculties. When we pray we can become aware of Jesus's hands being laid on us, we can experience his touch, his supporting grip, even his embrace. . . .

– Find a comfortable posture . . . close your eyes . . . and quieten yourself . . .

– Do one of the relaxation exercises . . .

– Become aware of the Holy Spirit living in you . . . ask him to guide you through this prayer . . . ask him to show you the hands of Jesus, the master of all true prayer . . .

– Become aware of the hands of Jesus, try to meditate and reflect upon them as fully as you can. They are the hands with which he worked for many years as a carpenter . . . During his public life these hands became very much hands of healing and blessing . . . the sick longed for them . . . they are the hands that Jesus constantly raised to heaven in prayer in order to lay them again on the sick to heal and console them . . .

– These are the hands with which he blessed the bread and handed it over to his Disciples that they in turn might distribute it to the hungry . . . At the Last

Supper these hands took the bread, blessed and broke it and it became himself for us all . . .

— These are the hands with which he touched and blessed so many people and things . . . they are the hands that have been pierced for us and which he then showed to his Apostles as a sign of his resurrection . . .

— His right hand grasped the hand of the blind man and led him away from the crowd into a peaceful place where he could heal him . . . with this same hand he took the hand of the mother-in-law of Peter in order to lift her up from her sick bed . . . with the same hand he got hold of the hand of the sinking Peter in order to save him from drowning . . . and he also clasped the little hand of the daughter of Jairus and called her back to life . . .

— When you feel the time is right, begin to close your prayer and thank God. . .

— Slowly and gently open your eyes and end the prayer.

"Jesus takes me by the hand"
(Matthew 14:22–36)

We often take each other's hand, and for various reasons. We may want to guide a person – who is blind or old, sick or handicapped. Or we may want to say: "Come with me, come on!" Sometimes we want to console a person, show our sympathy and concern for him; or we may want to say goodbye to someone we love and to give him courage for the journey; or it may be that we want to make peace and be reconciled with someone. Jesus must have often given someone his hand, not only on the occasions mentioned in the gospels, but at many other times. We can imagine that we are people of his time. He meets us too and takes our hands . . . We can do this reflecting on any gospel story, but it is perhaps more helpful to make use of a Bible story in which Jesus took somebody by the hand.

— Read slowly through the passage above. . . .

— Find a comfortable posture . . . close your eyes . . . and quieten yourself . . .

— Do one of the relaxation exercises . . .

— Become aware of the Holy Spirit living in you . . . ask him to guide you through this prayer experience . . . he is the master of all prayer . . .

— Become aware of Jesus . . . think of his hands . . . the people he touched by his hands and the people he took by the hand for various reasons . . .

— See yourself in your own situation . . . perhaps you too feel, as Peter did, that you have no more ground under your feet, and you cry out "Lord save me" . . . feel how he stretches out his hands and gets hold of you and pulls you out . . . feel his strong hands . . . take courage and have faith . . . stay as long as you can with the image of Jesus holding your hands and pulling you out of your trouble . . . Be aware that they are the hands of Jesus that hold you . . . the whole situation may then lighten, even though you may not consciously feel this at first . . .

— When you feel the time is right, begin to close your prayer and thank God. . .

— Slowly and gently open your eyes and end the prayer.

"And he was made clean"
(Matthew 8:1–14; Mark 1:40–45; Luke 5:12–16)

Sometimes we may become especially aware of our sinfulness, our broken-ness and woundedness. At such times we feel weighed down by our weakness, our imperfections and our deficiencies. Sometimes we have too heavy a load of guilt which we need to be freed from, or our hurts and sorrows go too deep. In the face of all this it might help us to recall how Jesus touched the leper with his hand and made him clean.

Remembering this healing touch of Jesus, we too can entrust ourselves to him and experience his love for us. At his touch he can liberate us from all that takes away our freedom, cleansing and healing us.

— Slowly read through one of the above passages. . . .

— Find a comfortable posture . . . close your eyes . . . and quieten yourself . . .

— Do one of the relaxation exercises . . .

— Become aware of the Holy Spirit living in you . . . ask him to guide you through this prayer experience . . . he is the real pray-er in you . . .

- Become aware of the hands of Jesus . . . think of the people they have touched and the healing they have brought them . . .

- Think specifically of the story of the leper . . . place yourself in his situation . . . What did he feel? . . . What did Jesus feel? . . . What did Jesus do? . . . and what happened? . . .

- See yourself as a leper covered and burdened with all kinds of things personal to you . . . Be aware of how Jesus has pity on you . . . he takes your hand and lays his hand on you . . . feel his touch . . . be aware that Jesus himself is touching you . . . you the sinner . . . Let it seep into you . . . deep, very deep, that Jesus touches you . . . be aware that he has cleansed the leper, so he can also heal you . . . Just rest in this awareness for as long as you can . . .

- When you feel the time is right, begin to close your prayer and thank God. . .

- Slowly and gently open your eyes and end the prayer.

"Jesus embraces us from the cross"

In the House of Prayer at Burn Hall, two miles from Durham, we have a beautiful statue of Christ on the Cross with St Francis standing beneath it. Jesus bends down from the Cross and is about to embrace St Francis. Perhaps we may feel: "That's all right for St Francis, he was a saint, but I am just an ordinary person". But did Jesus not die for everyone? Is the love that is manifested

126

in his suffering and death not specially meant for us? If that is so, can we then not also look up at the Cross and humbly marvel at his mercy and goodness towards us? We may then see, "see" with our hearts, how Jesus frees his arms from the Cross and bends down to us, putting his arm around each one of us?

— Find a comfortable posture . . . close your eyes . . . and quieten yourself . . .

— Do one of the relaxation exercises . . .

— Become aware of the Holy Spirit living in you . . . ask him to guide you in this experience . . .

— Look at the Cross with your inner eye, the eye of the heart . . . look at Jesus . . . see his humility, his good-ness and his tremendous love . . . imagine that he bends down from the Cross and puts his arms around you . . . feel them around you . . . feel his embrace . . .

— Now rest in this embrace as long as you can . . . savour and relish it . . . and as ordinary person with your strengths and weaknesses, feel God's love for you and accept it; it is meant for *you* . . .

— When you feel the time is right, begin to close your prayer and thank God. . .

— Slowly and gently open your eyes and end the prayer.

"The Disciple whom Jesus loved, rested his head on the breast of Jesus"
(John 13:23)

We all know the scene of the Last Supper. St John tells us that the disciple whom Jesus loved was sitting on the left of Jesus and was resting his head on his breast. Many artists show us these two – John resting his head on the breast of Jesus, and Jesus holding with his right hand the right hand of John. He has his left arm around the shoulder of John. This gesture surely wants to tell John: "You are very secure." John's answer to this is that he holds the right hand of Jesus and rests his head on his chest and so feels very secure and safe.

God is love and Jesus has come into the world to demonstrate to us this love. Let us try to experience a bit of this great love through an exercise.

– Find a comfortable posture . . . close your eyes . . . and quieten yourself . . .

– Do one of the relaxation exercises . . .

– Become aware of the Holy Spirit living in you . . . ask him to guide you through this prayer experience . . .

– Imagine the scene of Jesus and John at the Last Supper . . . see the details and live yourself into the closeness of these two persons . . .

– Imagine you are with Jesus as John was at the Last Supper . . . imagine yourself sitting next to Jesus . . . rest your head on Jesus's breast . . . feel how he gets hold of your right hand and puts his left arm around your shoulder . . . feel his touch and his closeness . . . feel the comfort and security . . . feel at peace and at rest . . . don't worry about anything . . . just feel at home and loved and secure and let everything else go . . . stay with this as long as you can . . .

– When you feel the time is right, begin to close your prayer and thank God. . .

– Slowly and gently open your eyes and end the prayer.

PART EIGHT

Praying with the Sense of Sight

The saintly Curé d'Ars, who was a priest in the first half of the nineteenth century, had in his parish a man whom he saw regularly in the church, either on an evening during the week or on Sunday afternoon. He always found him sitting in the same place and he never gave the impression that he was praying. He just sat there looking straight ahead, often for more than an hour.

One day the Curé said to him: "What are you doing here? What prayer are you offering up?" The man answered; "What I am doing, whether it is prayer or not, I do not know. I just look at Jesus." The Curé replied: "You ask me whether what you are doing is prayer? It most certainly is. What you are doing is a very beautiful way of praying. We could give it the name contemplation." The man was puzzled by the word "contemplation" as he did not understand its meaning, but he was satisfied to know that his way of praying was pleasing to the Curé.

The word "contemplation" is in fact derived from Latin, meaning: To gaze upon, to look at, to admire, and that is precisely what the man was doing. I would like to say a few things here about contemplation and how it relates to our ordinary way of seeing and looking.

We can see things in many ways. We can see something without paying any attention to it, or we can specifically look out for something and when we catch sight of it proceed to look at it from all sides. We can examine it closely, admire it, marvel at it and try to assimilate it into ourselves and be filled with what we see. When the object in question is a person it is usually not necessary that we scrutinize and examine the person from all viewpoints. It is enough for us just to look at the person, and admire and love him or her.

Every normal person is capable of using his imagination; that which engages it originates in his memory. This means that objects we have seen in the past with our eyes are stored up in our memory, and at a later date we can bring them before our inner eye to see them interiorly.

We can also picture interiorly something that we have not actually seen. This happens when, for example, someone describes his holiday in a country we have never visited. By following his detailed and perhaps graphic description of the scenery, we can form a picture of the landscape in our imagination.

We do this by making use of pictures and images from our own memory of things and places already seen, such as lakes, valleys, meadows, trees, houses or animals. All we are doing is altering our memory a little and applying the images to the description we have heard, or placing them in a new setting. When we call to mind a beautiful experience we have had we see it in interior images. When we build castles in the air they appear before our inner eye in pictures. When we think of a beloved person we can often see him quite close to us, even though he may be very far off.

All this we can do in prayer, too; we call it praying imaginatively. We are not giving God something but, rather, we are perceiving something of him. If this inner seeing of religious images is real prayer then we can quite easily practise it.

In seeing things with our inner eyes, we should not try to examine the picture to try to understand all the minor details, but rather allow ourselves to be impressed by its *total* content. This is especially true when we see things prayerfully. In our prayer tradition this has often been called the "Prayer of Simple Gaze".

When a mother sits at the bedside of her sleeping child, she does not look continually at the face of the child in order to discover some signs of sickness or of re-semblance to the parents. More often than not she will simply gaze at the child – nothing more.

When we are confronted with the sight of something beautiful, such as a calm lake, a marvellous sunset or a beautiful flower, we experience feelings of marvel and wonder. We do not rack our brains to find out the name of the flower, why it grows there and what its purpose is. We simply look and experience a feeling of enjoyment, and we do this much more with our heart than with our head. This we can also do in prayer.

We have been speaking all the time of having images or pictures before our eyes as if this was the easiest of things. Some of us find this very hard to do and often we are unsuccessful in our attempts. The reason for this may be that our imagination is not very well developed, or it may be in the object we are trying to imagine. When we try to reproduce a picture of Jesus in our imagination we often do not know what sort of picture to conjure up. Should we try to imagine him looking like another human being or not? Often we are inhibited out of shyness. This is even more the case when we try to imagine a picture of God himself, who is invisible, and who therefore cannot

132

be imagined. Here we are confronted not only with the question – "May we make an image of God?" but also with – "Are we able to conjure up any image or picture of God?" So we have to keep in mind what it means to see, and what happens to us when we catch sight of something.

To see means to perceive or to become aware of an object. We become aware, or we recognize, that something, or someone, is in front of us and therefore present to us. This we can also do with God and Jesus. We need not see a figure in front of our inner eyes, for we can still be fully aware of his presence without seeing his figure. We can simply close our eyes and look into the empty space in front of us: In the middle of that empty space there stands God. Then we try to allow the faith that believes in his presence to become so vibrant and alive that we may feel like shouting – "Yes, I see you, O my God, I see you!" This is a real "seeing" – a "seeing" with the eyes of faith. We now look at him whom we know to be present before us.

In doing this, we need not ask any searching questions such as, "Where are you? or . . . What do you look like?" We simply let the eyes of our faith and our heart try to gaze at him anew, as if we can really see him.

The farmer told the Curé d'Ars that he looked at Jesus, but we can be certain that his looking had become a seeing – a long, quiet sitting with his eyes of faith and heart, fixed on the Lord in the tabernacle. He was a total receiver – a complete see–er – and this, so much so, that no other form of prayer suggested itself to him. No words were needed – it was just a matter of sitting and looking – nothing else.

"Look at the lilies of the field"
(Matthew 6:25–34)

Jesus tells us to look at the lilies of the field and the birds of the air. He tells us to look at them. But do we really ever look at them? Even if we do, we often hardly see them because our mind is not on them. Our minds are usually engaged on past events or those still to come. Very rarely do we concentrate on what we are *actually* looking at. So if, for example, you are walking along a country road, try to look at the grass and the birds or at the cows, the sheep or the horses. Look at them, savour and relish their beauty. This also holds good for those of you who live in towns and cities. There are usually parks to hand, large or small, containing flowers, trees and shrubs. These places contain sufficient natural life to nourish our minds and hearts.

As we look at them we must not think about them, just look, listen and be – like the flowers of the field and the birds of the air – just be there. How beautifully nature can teach us just to be. So, let us try to look and see first of all with our physical eyes but then go a step further and look also with our heart – heart-seeing.

So let us have a go at it: . . .

– Find a comfortable posture . . . close your eyes . . . and quieten yourself . . .

– Do one of the relaxation exercises . . .

– Become aware of the Holy Spirit living in you . . . ask him to help you to look with eyes that look through the heart . . .

– Gently take a rose, or any other flower, into your hand . . . look at it with soft eyes, as with eyes behind eyes . . .

134

— Continue to look gently, and contemplate it deeply . . . allow the rose to be itself: a rose, the handiwork of God . . .

— Do not analyze it but take the rose as a total being and gently and contemplatively allow it to be itself . . . Do not violate it . . . Allow it to be what it is: A rose . . .

— Now allow the rose slowly to withdraw . . . then rest in your own inner space, inner stillness, inner truth . . .

— When you feel the time is right, begin to close your prayer and thank God. . .

— Slowly and gently open your eyes and end the prayer.

A visit to a church

When we remember a beautiful experience we have had, we see it in interior images. When we build castles in the air they stand before our inner eyes in pictures. We can also do this in prayer. We can think of a visit to a church where we were very touched and moved by the beauty of the building and the beautiful service. We can experience this again interiorly and, once more, be touched in the heart and moved to praise God. . . .

— Find a comfortable posture . . . close your eyes . . . and quieten yourself . . .

— Do one of the relaxation exercises . . .

— Now become aware of the Holy Spirit living in you . . . ask him to guide you through this prayer experience

. . . ask him to open your inner eyes so that you may see and experience and be touched . . .

— Now think of a church that you have once visited, a church in which you were very much impressed and moved by its beauty and perhaps its atmosphere of prayer . . .

— Compose yourself and try to see the church again interiorly in your imagination . . . see the people, all that is happening, the prayer or the music, all that once impressed and moved you . . .

— Try to relive the whole experience again . . . allow yourself to be touched by all that you see and hear. Gaze at the beauty in this experience . . . feel close to God . . .

— When you feel the time is right, begin to close your prayer and thank God. . .

— Slowly and gently open your eyes and end the prayer.

See Jesus looking at you

St Teresa of Avila often told her sisters to look at Jesus and see him looking at them. It was a favourite form of praying for her. She says, "Look at him who is looking at you". She qualifies the way Jesus looks at us by drawing attention to two important adverbs: *lovingly* and *humbly*. Jesus looks at us: lovingly, that is, with love, and humbly, that is, with humility.

We may find this hard to believe. We don't want to see and admit that Jesus can look at us lovingly and humbly.

We have a too negative opinion of ourselves and a too harsh opinion of Jesus. He might look at us with love when we are very good and holy, yes, but how can he when we feel nothing like this? To look at us humbly, he the creator, the Son of God, the Saviour and Master! How can he look at us humbly?

Jesus is our servant and slave, the one who washes our feet. He has not come to be served but to serve. He willingly died for us on the Cross out of love for us. He became nothing for us out of love. Should this Jesus then not look at us lovingly and humbly? . . .

– Find a comfortable posture . . . close your eyes . . . and quieten yourself . . .

– Do one of the relaxation exercises . . .

– Become aware of the Holy Spirit living in you . . . ask him to guide you through this prayer experience . . . He is the Spirit of Jesus . . . He will help you to see Jesus with our inner eyes of love . . . and see him look at you lovingly and humbly . . . . .

– Imagine you see Jesus standing before you . . . He is looking at you . . . Notice the love in his look . . . Notice the humility . . .

– Look at him looking at you – allow yourself to be looked at . . . Humble yourself and allow yourself to be loved . . . Rest in this gaze of love as long as you can. Do not do anything or say anything . . . Let his loving and humble gaze be deeply imprinted in your heart . . .

– When you feel the time is right, begin to close your prayer and thank God. . .

– Slowly and gently open your eyes and end the prayer.

The Lord and the Servant

In the *Revelations of Divine Love* Julian of Norwich saw two persons in bodily form: a Lord and a Servant. The Lord was seated solemnly, at peace and at rest. The Servant was standing humbly near his Lord, ready to do his Lord's will. The Lord looked upon his Servant with love and great tenderness and humbly sent him away on an errand. The Servant not only went but immediately ran off at great speed and haste, so keen was he to do his Lord's will. But soon he fell into a ditch and hurt himself badly. He moaned and groaned, wailed and struggled, but he could not get up or help himself in any way. His greatest trial was that there was no comfort at hand, for he could not turn his face to look back and see the face of his loving Lord who was in fact very near to him and full of comfort. Instead he behaved weakly and foolishly for the time being and thought only of his suffering and distress.

But the loving Lord looked upon his servant most tenderly with a twofold attitude. Firstly, he regarded him very lovingly and gently, with great compassion and pity, not with blame. Then secondly, he greatly rejoiced thinking of how he would reward his servant. He said to himself: See my beloved servant here! See what harm and distress he has incurred while in service for love of me, yes, and see his good will! Is it, therefore, not proper that I should reward him for his fright and fear, his pain and his wounds and all his grief? And not only this, should I not also reward him with a gift that would serve him better and be more honourable to him than his own health would have been? What goodness! What a wonderful Lord! Even the falling and the grief which the servant has incurred, are to be turned into surpassing glory and endless joy. (Taken from Chapter 15.)

— Find a comfortable posture . . . close your eyes . . . and quieten yourself . . .

— Do one of the relaxation exercises . . .

— Become aware of the Holy Spirit living in you . . . ask him to guide you through this prayer . . . to let you see and experience what Julian saw, for he inspired her, and can also inspire you . . .

— Now see the Lord and the servant . . . look at them closely . . . look at their expressions, their attitudes, their dress . . .

— Look at the servant dashing off to do the Lord's will . . . see him fall and see him in his miserable state . . . look at him closely . . . observe him, see yourself in him . . .

— Now look at the Lord . . . see his face . . . his expression . . . do you see any anger, any blame in him? . . . see the goodness, love, compassion and pity that radiate from his face . . . See how he wants to reward the servant for his pain and suffering . . .

— Admire this Lord . . . bathe yourself in his goodness and mercy . . . See God in him . . . see yourself as sinner in the servant . . . and just rest in the love and goodness of the Lord . . .

— When you feel the time is right, begin to close your prayer and thank God. . .

— Slowly and gently open your eyes and end the prayer.

Simeon and the child
(Luke 2:22–35)

The possibilities of praying imaginatively with our inner eyes are infinite. We can, for instance, allow someone to tell us a story of something that we have not experienced ourselves, but which we ourselves can then experience through the help of our imagination. Let us here take the story of the prophet Simeon and the child Jesus in the Temple:

– Read slowly through the above passage . . .

– Find a comfortable posture . . . close your eyes . . . and quieten yourself . . .

– Do one of the relaxation exercises . . .

– Become aware of the Holy Spirit living in you . . . ask him to guide you . . . ask him to help you see and experience what Simeon saw and experienced . . .

– Place yourself in the temple at Jerusalem . . . see the place . . . the people . . . see Simeon and Joseph and Mary and the child . . .

– See Simeon taking the child in his arms . . . watch his face, his expression and see the joy that radiates from his face . . . see how he looks at the child that he holds in his arms . . . just watch him . . .

– Take the child into your own arms and look at him . . . see his face . . . Just look at the face and keep on doing so . . . savour and relish it like a mother who enjoys looking at the face of her little child . . . look at it as long as you can . . . you will see many things in this little

140

face and it will reveal to you many things . . . just look, admire, and love . . .

— Now give the child back to the mother and say something to her and the child . . .

— When you feel the time is right, begin to close your prayer and thank God. . .

— Slowly and gently open your eyes and end the prayer.

Jesus on the Cross

Many people have told me that they never see an image when they pray, but we don't necessarily need to. It is enough to focus our attention on him whom we want to see. When we do this, then very often our mind will also produce, before our inner eyes, a real image of him whom we are looking at in faith.

For instance, we look at Jesus as he hangs on the Cross. We only think of and imagine what we might see were the crucifixion taking place here and now. In the course of our imaginative reflection, our attention becomes more and more centred on what is happening on Calvary, and thus we cannot fail to see with our inner eyes of love and faith what we have been thinking about so intensely.

— Find a comfortable posture . . . close your eyes . . . and quieten yourself . . .

— Do one of the relaxation exercises . . .

141

— Become aware of the Holy Spirit living in you . . . ask him to guide you, to pray in you and open your eyes of faith and love so that you may "see" with your heart . . .

— Place yourself on Calvary . . . familiarize yourself with the situation . . . see what is going on there . . .

— Concentrate even more on Jesus on the Cross and focus your whole heart, your whole love and faith on him . . . keep on looking at him, with faith and love . . . Try not to get side-tracked by accidentals . . . keep on looking at Jesus . . . and stay with this as long as you can . . .

— When you feel the time is right, begin to close your prayer and thank God. . .

— Slowly and gently open your eyes and end the prayer.

PART NINE

Praying with Scripture

It was while I was a missionary in Borneo that I really began to fall in love with the Word of God. During my years studying theology I had not felt this attraction nor did I experience its power and influence on peoples lives. Instead, this grace was given to me through seeing how deeply it affected a young man I came to know on my missionary travels.

While in charge of Lay Ministries in the diocese, I had to go around to the parishes conducting seminars and giving talks. It was while giving a talk on the Word of God that I had the following experience. Among those attending the seminar was a young man of about thirty years. He was married and had three children, and I learned that he had only recently become a Christian. He was so eager to know more about this new-found faith that the parish priest sent him to the seminar. I noticed how attentive he was and how eagerly he listened to what I said about the Word of God. He had never attended school and could read only a little, so I gave him a New Testament in his own language. On receiving it his whole face lit up. Throughout the day I could see him clasping his book wherever he went. It became his treasure – a priceless pearl.

A few months later it was discovered that he had terminal cancer. He did not live very long after that. But meanwhile the Word of God and prayer were his painkillers. The Bible was near at hand at all times and it was the source of his strength, his power and his joy. It meant more than anything else to him, and as the days went on he was able to detach himself from everything else, even his wife and children whom he loved very dearly. The only thing he clung to till the very end was his Bible. He died with it on his chest and was buried with it. This man was indeed good soil for the Word of God. In him it could take root and bear fruit. Is not this the very reason why the Word of God was written down? St John tells us in 20:31: "These words are written that you may believe that Jesus is the Christ, the Son of God, and that, believing, you may have life in his name".

In the world in which we live it is very difficult for God to communicate to us. God has a struggle to make his voice heard, in order that his message will sink in, take root and bear fruit that will last.

Take for example the Word of God spoken to Isaiah (43:1–4): "I have redeemed you, I have called you by your name. You are mine . . . you are precious in my eyes, you are honoured and I love you." How can these and similar words of God become so rooted in us, that their spirit and life fills us with the unshakable convictions that we really do belong, that we have immense value and are worthy of honour and, above all, that we are loved, and are God's delight and joy?

There are many ways and methods that help us to take in the Word of God, to digest it and then try to live it out in our lives. Here I am suggesting yet another form of praying the Word of God.

After the now-familiar opening of the prayer experience, the Word of God can probe and cut its way right through into the core of our being and we are then open to its changing and transforming us. It can develop new attitudes in us, new ways of relating to people and to the world. It can affect our whole life, the way we think, the way we speak and the way we behave, but don't worry if it does not do this all at once!

So, after the general lead into the experience, we take up the "*Word*" that we have chosen to pray with and let it penetrate our mind. We let the Word come to life in us, in all its richness. We let it become rooted, alive and active in the thinking part of our being. We need not spend too much time in trying to *understand* the Word. We just take it in, and let it live in us.

In this chapter the "Word of God" refers mainly to a biblical quote from the Bible containing many words. In it Paul speaks to us, to each one of us personally. We repeat it interiorly, to extract from it all its spiritual essence. It cannot yield all the sap that it contains at once, for this must be drawn out slowly to the last drop. So we must come back to the same Word again and again, and we must let it resound, echo in us for as long as it is necessary for it to bear fruit, to nourish our mind.

So far we have taken the Word of God into our mind. Now we must take it into our heart, so that its spirit and life and attitude may penetrate to the very core of our being, and become alive and active in our blood and in our bones. In the heart it will meet the Spirit who first inspired it and He will bring it to life and make it bear fruit.

If we dare to take God at his word, we are bound to discover that, deep down, we are precious and highly honoured people – people so lovable that Jesus could die for us. The Word of God, always and inevitably, speaks from the centre of the Cross: "You are precious and I love You."

So far we have reflected on the Word of God in our mind, and we have savoured and relished it in our heart. It has made a deep impression on us. Like the surgeon's knife, it has penetrated to the core of our intellectual and emotional life.

In the Gospel, Jesus tells us that if we want to keep our life, we must be prepared to give it away, otherwise we will lose it. What we try to hold on to, to grasp with our hands, we will lose. Only when we share with others will we retain it. So we can never keep the gifts of God to ourselves. They must be shared with others. The Word which has been impressed on our mind and heart must be shared. Contemplative living can never be just a matter of thoughts and feelings; it must be a life of thoughts, feelings and deeds. The sign of real growth and maturing in us is seen in what we do; in the way we look at people and at the world; in the way we speak to people; in the way we behave and treat them, and, too, in the way we treat and care for ourselves.

So far, the Lord has tried to impress his Word upon us, the Good News of his desire for our well-being. If we have taken the Lord seriously, and tried to allow him to touch us with his Word, then this will have left its mark on us. We shall therefore have the same kind of longing for others as the Lord has, whether we feel it or not. We shall want to share his Word, the Good News. We love because we have been loved. We want to heal because we have been healed. We want to forgive because we have been forgiven. We want to give value and worth to others because we have been given a deep sense of value and worth. We want to help, to encourage and lift up, because he has done all this to us. In short, the Word of God's love

can become our word of love. His vocabulary and attitude can become ours. "You are mine . . . you are precious in my eyes . . . I honour you and I love you . . ."

At this stage in our prayer we are now ready to give our
time and attention to other people and to the world as a
whole, using our imagination to the full. We picture at
first our own family, our community or some individual
friend. We see them in their various situations and
difficulties, in their needs and dangers. We try to understand their circumstances. For this we must take time and
care. As we see these people before us, and look at them,
or rather look into them and feel their needs, we should
begin to share in God's desire and longing for them. We
have experienced God's love. We have heard his word
and it has touched us, helped us, healed us, and encour-
aged us. It has lifted us up, forgiven us and given us new
hope. It has changed and transformed us. It has done all
this to us. So now we should have the same desire and
longing as God, to share these priceless words with
others. In our imagination we say them to the people
before us. We say them with the same conviction and
desire as the Lord. We put ourselves into them: "Peter
you are precious to me . . . I love you . . ." We do this for
a while, then we rest in this thought.

We can also take a whole parish, or society, and look at
it. As we think about and feel for the people, we will know
the ways in which they need to come alive, ways in which
the Word of God needs to penetrate to the very core of
their worship and mission; perhaps ways in which they
fail to obey the Lord's command to love one another. It
could even be that a particular member is a source of
trouble. Yet God loves them all and he longs for the well-
being of them all. So again we share in this desire of the

Lord and speak the Lord's Word to them. We want to see them all alive, active and well, as the Lord does. We can share in his desire and longing.

Even if the people cornered cannot hear our voice, do not know of our desire and longing for them, do not feel the touch of our hands, and are not aware that we are praying for them, this will still have a tremendous effect on them. But even if it does not help others, at least it helps us. We will begin to sense, feel, live and suffer with people. We will begin to feel ourselves more at one with them, and rejoice and suffer with them. Jesus has become one with us, we must become one with them.

In this way we could go on using the God-given gift of imagination, achieving a vision of his concern for the life of our nation, the world and the whole of creation, sharing something of his immense and loving desire that all things be well. I think this could be a real contemplative way of praying for others. We could be immersed and lost in this infinite desire and longing of God for the salvation of the whole world. If we pray this way every day, we will see what difference it makes to our life. It will give us a sense of personal well-being, which floods into all our doings, and will affect all our environment. This is so, because the Word of God will be at work in us and express itself through us. "Everyone who hears these words of mine and does them, will be like a wise man who built his house on a rock" (Matthew 7:24).

"Do not let your hearts be troubled. Have faith in God and faith in me"

- Find a comfortable posture . . . close your eyes . . . and quieten yourself . . .

- Do one of the relaxation exercises . . .

- Now become aware of the Holy Spirit living in you . . . ask him to lead and guide you through this prayer . . .

- Bring the word that you have chosen for this prayer experience to your mind: "Do not let your hearts be troubled. Have faith in God and faith in me" . . . Say the word several times . . . Assimilate it into your mind . . . reflect on it . . . Become aware of its meaning to you especially if you are at the moment feeling troubled . . . After some time stop . . . and savour the message for a while . . .

- Now you must take the word to your heart . . . Impress it there, so that its life and spirit may penetrate the very core of your being . . . In your heart, it will meet the Spirit . . . He will make it develop and bear fruit . . . So speak the word again several times: "Do not let your hearts be troubled. Have faith in God and faith in me" . . .

Let the word echo in your heart . . . Enjoy it . . . Let your feelings and imagination play their part . . . After a time, stop . . . and rest in the well-being the word has given you . . .

- Now you must give the word to others . . . You must give it away if you want to keep it . . . The Lord loves you . . . He wants you to be at peace and full of joy . . .

So he spoke the beautiful words to you . . . He now wants you to say them to others . . .

— Let some people come before you . . . See their needs, their fears, troubles and despair . . . Have pity on them . . . Look at them with the eyes of Jesus, and say to them: "Do not let your hearts be troubled. Have faith in God and faith in me" . . . Say them as Jesus said them to you . . .

— When you feel the time is right, begin to close your prayer and thank God . . .

— Slowly and gently open your eyes and end the prayer.

"Heal me Lord and I shall be healed, save me and I shall be saved"
(Jeremiah 17:14)

— Find a comfortable posture . . . close your eyes . . . and quieten yourself . . .

— Do one of the relaxation exercises . . .

— Become aware of the Holy Spirit living in you . . . ask him to guide you through this prayer experience . . . ask him to pray in you, through and with you . . .

— Bring the word that you have chosen for this prayer experience to your mind. "Heal me Lord and I shall be healed, save me and I shall be saved" . . . Say the word several times . . . Implant it into your mind . . . Ponder on it . . . Become aware of its meaning for you . . .

When you feel it right stop saying the word, and rest in its truth . . .

— Now take the word to your heart . . . Impress it there, so that its life and spirit may penetrate the very core of your being . . . In your heart it will meet the Spirit . . . He will make it grow, and bear fruit . . . So speak the word again several times:

"Heal me Lord and I shall be healed,
Save me and I shall be saved" . . .

Let the words penetrate right into your heart . . . Enjoy them . . . Let your feelings and imagination be touched by them . . . How do you feel? . . . What does the word of God do to you? . . . How does it affect you? . . . Respond to it in the way you feel . . . After a time, when you feel it is right, stop repeating the word, and rest in the feeling of well-being which it has brought you . . .

— Now you must express the word to others . . . If you want to keep the word, you must first give it away . . . The grain in order to bear fruit must first die . . . The Lord love you . . . He wants to heal you and to save you . . . He wants to see you whole . . . So he spoke these words to you . . . They touched you, and gave you hope and confidence . . . So now try to do the same to others . . .

Let the people you want to pray for come before you . . . See their sickness, their brokenness, hear their cry for help. Have pity on them and say to them the Word of

God . . . Say the words with the same love and compassion as the Lord has said them to you . . . Trust in the word you are saying . . . Say it several times . . . keep on saying it for as long as you feel comfortable . . . When you feel you ought to, stop and rest in God . . .

— When you feel the time is right, begin to close your prayer and thank God. . .

— Slowly and gently open your eyes and end the prayer.

"I came that you may have life, and have it abundantly"

— Find a comfortable posture . . . close your eyes . . . and quieten yourself . . .

— Do one of the relaxation exercises . . .

— Become aware of the Holy Spirit living in you . . . ask him to guide you through this prayer experience . . . to pray in you . . .

— Bring the Word of God that you have chosen to your mind: "I came that you may have life, and have it abundantly" . . . Repeat the word over and over in your mind . . . let it become alive . . . Become aware of what the word means to you . . . Notice the various images and associations . . . Store it up there and express it firmly . . . After a time stop repeating the word and rest in the wealth of truth that it has given you.

— Now take the word to your heart . . . You must express it there too, so that its life and spirit may penetrate the

152

very core of your being . . . The Spirit will make it grow and bear fruit . . .

Repeat the word . . . "I came that you may have life, and have it abundantly" . . . Rejoice in it . . . Let your feelings and imagination take part in the joy of this great message . . . After a time stop and rest in the peace and joy that this Word gives you . . .

— If you want to keep the word you must give it away . . . The word has made you more like God . . . He has given you his life . . . You live now by it . . . He gave himself away for you . . . So now you must do the same . . . by sharing your life with others . . .

Let the people that you want to pray for, come before you . . . See their needs, their divisions, and longings . . . Help them . . . reach out to them . . . offer them the life of God . . . Speak to them the Word God has spoken to you . . . "I came that you may have life . . . " Then rest and let the word of God make them fully alive . . .

— When you feel the time is right, begin to close your prayer and thank God. . .

— Slowly and gently open your eyes and end the prayer.

"If you make my word your home, you will indeed be my disciples"
(John 8:31)

— Find a comfortable posture . . . close your eyes . . . and quieten yourself . . .

— Do one of the relaxation exercises . . .

153

— Become aware of the Holy Spirit living in you . . . ask him to guide you through this prayer experience . . .

— Bring the Word of God that you have chosen to your mind: "If you make my word your home, you will indeed be my disciples."
Repeat the word over and over . . . Let it become alive . . . be aware of what it means to you . . . Notice the various images and associations . . . You need not analyze deeply . . . Just take the word with all its associations into your mind . . . Store it up there and impress it firmly . . . After a time stop repeating the Word and rest in the wealth of the truth that it has given you . . .

— Now you must take the Word to your heart . . . You must impress it there too, so that its life and spirit may penetrate the very core of your being . . . Where it will meet the Spirit . . . He will make it grow and bear fruit . . .
Repeat the Word . . . "If you make my word your home, you will indeed be my disciples" . . . Rejoice in the Word . . . It is so simple to be his disciples . . . Just love his Word and carry it out . . . After a time stop repeating the Word and rest in the peace and joy that it gives you . . .

— You must now try to give the Word away . . . The Word has made you more like Jesus . . . He shared his word with you and now you must share it with others . . .
Let the people you want to pray for come before you . . . Watch them . . . See their needs, their emptiness their search and hunger for God's word . . . So try to give it to them! . . . Speak to them the Word God has spoken to you . . . Impress it into their mind and heart . . . Keep on saying it . . . then rest and let it work in them . . .

— When you feel the time is right, begin to close your prayer and thank God. . .

— Slowly and gently open your eyes and end the prayer.

"I am the bread of life"

— Find a comfortable posture . . . close your eyes . . . and quieten yourself . . .

— Do one of the relaxation exercises . . .

— Become aware of the Holy Spirit living in you . . . ask him to guide you through this prayer experience . . .

— Now repeat the words: "I am the bread of life, He who comes to me shall not hunger, He who believes in me shall not thirst" . . . Let this Word of God come to life in your mind in all its richness . . . Take it all in . . . Repeat the Word over and over . . . Do not analyze it . . . Just take the meaning into your mind . . .

— Now you must take the Word to your heart so that its spirit and life may penetrate the very core of your being . . . In your heart it will find again the Spirit that inspired it in the first place . . . He will fertilize it and make it grow and bear fruit . . .

So bring the word down to your heart . . . Receive it open-heartedly because it feeds you, it quenches your thirst and gives you life . . . Let it work on your emotions and then rest in the peace and well-being it brings . . .

— You can only keep the Word by giving it away! The Word has made you more like Jesus . . . It has given

155

you his longing to feed your brothers and sisters, to quench their thirst and to give them life, so put it into practice . . .

Picture your family or friends or community, in front of you . . . watch them . . . water their hunger and thirst . . . then speak the Word of God to them which he has spoken to you . . . Wish to them what the Word meant to you . . . Do this for a while and then rest in the thought . . .

— When you feel the time is right, begin to close your prayer and thank God. . .

— Slowly and gently open your eyes and end the prayer.

"You are the salt of the earth you are the light of the world"
(Matthew 5:13–14)

— Find a comfortable posture . . . close your eyes . . . and quieten yourself . . .

— Do one of the relaxation exercises . . .

— Become aware of the Holy Spirit living in you . . . ask him to guide you through this prayer experience . . .

— Bring the Word of God that you have chosen for this prayer experience to your mind: "You are the salt of the earth, you are the light of the world" . . . Repeat the Word several times . . . Let it become alive in you . . . Become aware of what it means . . . Take note of the various images and associations that come to you . . . Store it up in your mind . . . After some time, stop

156

repeating the Word and then rest in the truth and understanding that it has given you . . .

— Now you must take the Word to your heart . . . Impress it there, so that its life, spirit and attitude may penetrate to the very core of your being . . . There it will meet the Spirit . . . who will make it grow and bear fruit . . . Repeat the word: "You are the salt of the earth, you are the light of the world" . . . Treasure the Word . . . Let it penetrate into your heart . . . Let your feelings and imagination take part . . . How does the word affect you? . . . How does it make you feel? . . . Love the Word . . . Be grateful for it and respond to it . . . After a time stop repeating it and rest in the feeling it has given you . . .

— Now you must express the Word . . . If you want to keep it, you must first give it away . . . The Lord loves you . . . He has told you a truth . . . He told you how he sees you . . . He wants you to be even more his image and likeness . . . So he was teaching you and inviting you . . . Now you should try to have the same longing for others . . . So speak this Word of God to others . . .

— Let the people you want to pray for come before you . . . Watch them . . . See their needs, their inferiority complexes, their feelings of unworthiness, love them and say the Word of God to them, and so give them courage and hope . . . Repeat it to them, then rest . . . Let the Word do its work . . .

— When you feel the time is right, begin to close your prayer and thank God. . .

— Slowly and gently open your eyes and end the prayer.

"If you ask anything of the Father in my name, He will give it to you"
(John 16:23)

- Find a comfortable posture . . . close your eyes . . . and quieten yourself . . .

- Do one of the relaxation exercises . . .

- Become aware of the Holy Spirit living in you . . . ask him to guide you through this prayer experience . . . to pray in you, through you . . .

- Now repeat the Word that you have chosen in your mind: "If you ask anything of the Father in my name, He will give it to you" . . . Say the Word several times . . . Let it penetrate your mind . . . Reflect on it . . . Become aware of the various images and associations it brings to you . . . Store it up in your mind . . . After a time stop saying the Word, and then rest in the truth and understanding that it has given you . . .

- Now you must try to take the Word to your heart . . . Impress it there, so that its life and spirit may penetrate the very core of your being . . . where it will meet the Spirit . . . He will make it develop and bear fruit . . . So repeat several times: "If you ask anything of the Father in my name, He will give it to you" . . . let it resound in your heart . . . Enjoy it . . . Let your feelings and imagination take part . . .

- Now you must express the Word . . . Remember if you want to keep and treasure it, you must first give it away . . . The Lord has done the same . . . Because he loves you, he has told you a great truth which has made you

158

happy and given you hope . . . So try to do the same for others . . .

Let the people you want to pray for, or the people the Holy Spirit brings to you, come before you . . . See their needs, their poverty, their desires . . . Have pity on them, and say to them the Word Jesus has just said to you . . . Keep on saying it to them . . . then rest in Jesus, and long that they may accept the Word . . .

— When you feel the time is right, begin to close your prayer and thank God. . .

— Slowly and gently open your eyes and end the prayer.

"You will seek me and find me when you seek me with all your heart"

— Find a comfortable posture . . . close your eyes . . . and quieten yourself . . .

— Do one of the relaxation exercises . . .

— Become aware of the Holy Spirit living in you . . . ask him to guide you through this prayer experience . . . ask him to pray in you, through and with you . . .

— Bring the Word of God that you have chosen to your mind: "You will seek me and find me, when you seek me with all your heart." Say it several times . . . Take it deeply into your mind . . . Reflect on its meaning . . . When you are saturated, stop saying it, and rest in the truth of this Word . . .

— Now you must take the word to your heart . . . Impress it there so that its life and spirit may penetrate the very core of your being . . . where it will meet the Spirit, who will make it grow and bear fruit . . .

Repeat the Word again several times, "You will seek me and find me when you seek me with all your heart." Let it penetrate your heart . . . Enjoy it . . . Let your feelings and imagination be touched by it . . .

After a time, stop repeating the Word and rest in the feeling of well-being which the Word has brought you . . .

– Now you must express the Word to others . . . If you want to keep the Word for yourself and treasure it, you must first give it away . . .

Let the people for whom you want to pray, or the people the Holy Spirit brings to you, come before you . . . See their desire and longings, their doubts and despair . . . Have pity on them and say to them the Word God has just spoken to you . . . with the same love and conviction as God said it to you . . . Believe what you are saying and keep on saying it, then rest in God and let the Word do its work . . .

– When you feel the time is right, begin to close your prayer and thank God. . .

– Slowly and gently open your eyes and end the prayer.

Conclusion

In the foregoing pages I have given you several ways with examples of how to pray contemplatively. Perhaps you have discovered one that suits you and you would like to form your future prayer life around that. As a conclusion, therefore, I would like to mention a very useful idea for you to take along on your journey into a more contemplative prayer life.

If you really want to live a contemplative *prayer* life it would be very helpful if you could also live your *daily* life more contemplatively. Our society has discovered many time-saving devices. This has certainly given us some material advantages and increased profits, but it has also impoverished us. We have become deprived of room and time to daydream, reflect, wonder and pray while working.

When Jesus was a carpenter he had to do all his work by hand as he had no modern equipment. He must have had plenty of room and time to wonder, reflect and pray. If modern carpenters let their concentration lapse even for a short time they might lose a few fingers. There were neither lorries nor tractors in those days, and so horses and oxen and other animals did the hauling. Those who led the animals had plenty of time to daydream, reflect and pray. Our grandmothers would also have had to fetch water from a well. They would wash clothes by hand and sweep floors with a broom, and all this would give them time to ponder over words and events from the Bible, just as Mary must have done.

There were also the long evenings when a mother would be busy with chores and the father would perhaps smoke his pipe and do a bit of reading. The little ones would be in bed while the older ones would be doing their home-work or enjoying their hobbies. There was neither TV nor radio. Now and then a few words might be spoken but for the rest there was silence.

In the summer evenings people would sit out in the garden, and during the cold winter nights they would sit around the fire. There would also be the long walks to church, to school and to buy things. All this and much more provided ample opportunities for meditation. People had time and opportunity to reflect and to pray.

Most of those opportunities have been taken away from us. This has made us very poor because we *do* need time to reflect, and to pray. This poverty can be seen in much of our behaviour and way of thinking. So are we totally orphaned? Are there really no more opportunities to be silent and engage in prayer? Yes, there are still such opportunities if we look for them and are able to make use of them.

In recent years various methods of meditation have been introduced from the East into our culture. These provide the very same opportunities our forbearers had – space and time in our lives. They advise us to concentrate on something simple, for instance on counting, or on repeating over and over again a simple word or phrase full of meaning, or just a word like Abba, Jesus, God.

We could concentrate on our breathing or on sitting still. We could also repeat prayers which we have learned by heart when young, or say the Rosary fingering our beads. All these activities occupy only a part of the mind, leaving the deeper part free for reflection, wonderment and contemplation.

162

There are also some more secular activities that can help achieve those ends and make us more conscious of the image of God. Such activities might include gardening, cooking, cycling, walking, skiing, picnicking and so on. Though these activities are not prayerful in themselves, we can use them for relaxation, for reflection and for prayer.

Our forefathers did this constantly by sanctifying certain everyday activities. The Celts, for example, had blessings and invocations for activities such as waking up, lighting the fire, eating breakfast, milking the cows. The same applied to fishing, planting, harvesting, resting and also dying. Our ancestors seldom separated their daily activities from an awareness of God's all-pervading presence. One can always be in contact with God, who is present in all things and events. But today, we may not be able to imitate our ancestors in all things, though we can still try to sanctify some of our more simple activities. This may just mean saying a simple prayer that we like. It can be without words, just becoming aware of God's presence in the work we are doing or an event we are part of. By doing this we can transform our activities into prayer.

Sunday would be a suitable time for such contemplative experiences. Sunday should be different from other days. It should be a more restful day, one that integrates our activities with our awareness of God's presence, although perhaps for the busy mother this is not always as easy as it sounds! On Sundays we don't all engage in full-time work. We should try to do only what we like to do, activities that are light and easy so that they can free our minds for reflection, and prayer.

163

It is during such meditative moments, when we have been able to find them, that we may hear God speaking to us. As we see in the Old Testament, God's voice is heard not in the thunder but in a whisper. These whispers or thoughts may flash through our mind as we daydream, coming apparently from nowhere. Or they may arise from something read or heard. God may be speaking to us in all those ways but to hear him we must be *listening*. This, of course, doesn't mean straining our ears. It does mean that we must try to still the turmoil of the mind and let it be receptive, for it is only then that we can hear God's whisper.

If we become aware of the various simple activities that do not fully occupy our mind, and make use of them to allow God to speak to us, we may at times experience God's influence leading us into prayer. Prayer is his gift. We cannot produce it, for God is the ground of all our prayer.

If we make ourselves available and receptive, and prepare ourselves, then God will give us this gift. Making use of such simple activities is an important step towards a more contemplative way of living and of praying. A contemplative way of life, which simply means to be aware and alert to God's presence in and around us, will surely lead us to a more contemplative prayer life.

I wish and pray that this book may be a great help to you in your prayer life. But remember, the only thing that is really important in prayer is: **"Love"**. God's love for us. All the rest will follow.